THE ENCYCLOPEDIA OF PSYCHOACTIVE DRUGS

IN 25 VOLUMES
Each title on a specific drug or drug-related problem

ALCOHOL
Alcohol And Alcoholism
Alcohol Customs & Rituals
Alcohol Teenage Drinking

HALLUCINOGENS
Flowering Plants Magic in Bloom
LSD Visions or Nightmares
Marijuana Its Effects on Mind & Body
Mushrooms Psychedelic Fungi
PCP The Dangerous Angel

NARCOTICS
Heroin The Street Narcotic
Methadone Treatment for Addiction
Prescription Narcotics The Addictive Painkillers

NON-PRESCRIPTION DRUGS
Over-the-Counter Drugs Harmless or Hazardous?

SEDATIVE HYPNOTICS
Barbiturates Sleeping Potion or Intoxicant?
Inhalants The Toxic Fumes
Quaaludes The Quest for Oblivion
Valium The Tranquil Trap

STIMULANTS
Amphetamines Danger in the Fast Lane
Caffeine The Most Popular Stimulant
Cocaine A New Epidemic
Nicotine An Old-Fashioned Addiction

UNDERSTANDING DRUGS
The Addictive Personality
Escape from Anxiety and Stress
Getting Help Treatments for Drug Abuse
Treating Mental Illness
Teenage Depression and Drugs

GENERAL EDITOR
Professor Solomon H. Snyder, M.D.
*Distinguished Service Professor of
Neuroscience, Pharmacology, and Psychiatry at
The Johns Hopkins University School of Medicine*

ASSOCIATE EDITOR
Professor Barry L. Jacobs, Ph.D.
Program in Neuroscience, Department of Psychology, Princeton University

SENIOR EDITORIAL CONSULTANT
Jerome H. Jaffe, M.D.
Director of The Addiction Research Center, National Institute on Drug Abuse

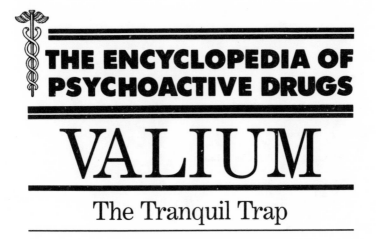

THE ENCYCLOPEDIA OF PSYCHOACTIVE DRUGS

VALIUM

The Tranquil Trap

GAIL WINGER, Ph.D.

University of Michigan

1986
CHELSEA HOUSE PUBLISHERS
NEW YORK
NEW HAVEN   PHILADELPHIA

COVER COLLAGE: Joan Hall, © 1983

SENIOR EDITOR: William P. Hansen
ASSOCIATE EDITORS: John Haney, Richard S. Mandell
ASSISTANT EDITORS: Paula Edelson, Perry Scott King
CAPTIONS: Jeff Freiert
EDITORIAL COORDINATOR: Karyn Gullen Browne
ART DIRECTOR: Susan Lusk
ART COORDINATOR: Carol McDougall
LAYOUT: Victoria Tomaselli
ART ASSISTANT: Noreen M. Lamb
PICTURE RESEARCH: Matt Miller

First printing

Library of Congress Cataloging in Publication Data
Winger, Gail.
    Valium : the tranquil trap.
    (The Encyclopedia of psychoactive drugs)
    Bibliography: p.
    Includes index.
    Summary: Examines the nature, effects, and dangers
of use and abuse of Valium and related anti-anxiety drugs.
    1. Benzodiazepine abuse—Juvenile literature.
2. Diazepam—Analysis—Juvenile literature. 3. Diazepam
—Toxicology—Juvenile literature. [1. Diazepam.
2. Benzodiazepine abuse. 3. Drugs. 4. Drug abuse]
I. Title. II. Series.
RC568.B45W56 1986   616.86'3   86-1282

ISBN 0-87754-759-9

Chelsea House Publishers
Harold Steinberg, Chairman & Publisher
Susan Lusk, Vice President
A Division of Chelsea House Educational Communications, Inc.

133 Christopher Street, New York, NY 10014

345 Whitney Avenue, New Haven, CT 05510

5014 West Chester Pike, Edgemont, PA 19028

Photos Courtesy of AP/Wide World Photos, Art Resource, Ayerst Laboratories, Hoff-
mann-LaRoche Inc., Fitz Hugh Ludlow Memorial Library, New York Academy of
Medicine, UPI/Bettmann Newsphotos, The Upjohn Company.

CONTENTS

Foreword 9
Introduction... 13
1 Anxiety and the Minor Tranquilizers..................................... 19
2 Beyond Anxiety: The Many Uses of Benzodiazepines.................. 43
3 How Dangerous Are the Minor Tranquilizers?........................ 53
4 Patterns of Tranquilizer Use... 71
5 Coping with Anxiety: Tranquilizers and Their Alternatives........... 81
6 Economic Issues and Prescribing Practices 91
7 Conclusion... 101
Appendix 1: How to Tell If Someone Has a Valium Problem............. 104
Appendix 2: Rules for Safer Use of Valium 105
Appendix 3: State Agencies 106
Further Reading... 113
Glossary.. 114
Index 118

Throngs of New Yorkers hurrying across the Brooklyn Bridge during a subway strike. The stress of urban living is but one reason why 20 million Americans currently take benzodiazepines such as Valium.

FOREWORD

In the Mainstream of American Life

The rapid growth of drug use and abuse is one of the most dramatic changes in the fabric of American society in the last 20 years. The United States has the highest level of psychoactive drug use of any industrialized society. It is 10 to 30 times greater than it was 20 years ago.

According to a recent Gallup poll, young people consider drugs the leading problem that they face. One of the legacies of the social upheaval of the 1960s is that psychoactive drugs have become part of the mainstream of American life. Schools, homes, and communities cannot be "drug proofed." There is a demand for drugs—and the supply is plentiful. Social norms have changed and drugs are not only available—they are everywhere.

Almost all drug use begins in the preteen and teenage years. These years are few in the total life cycle, but critical in the maturation process. During these years adolescents face the difficult tasks of discovering their identity, clarifying their sexual roles, asserting their independence, learning to cope with authority, and searching for goals that will give their lives meaning. During this intense period of growth, conflict is inevitable and the temptation to use drugs is great. Drugs are readily available, adolescents are curious and vulnerable, there is peer pressure to experiment, and there is the temptation to escape from conflicts.

No matter what their age or socioeconomic status, no group is immune to the allure and effects of psychoactive drugs. The U.S. Surgeon General's report, "Healthy People," indicates that 30% of all deaths in the United States

Mobs of shoppers in a department store. The hectic pace of modern society explains in part the high occurrence of anxiety and use of tranquilizers—according to the National Institute of Mental Health, over 13 million Americans suffer from some type of anxiety disorder.

are premature because of alcohol and tobacco use. However, the most shocking development in this report is that mortality in the age group between 15 and 24 has increased since 1960 despite the fact that death rates for all other age groups have declined in the 20th century. Accidents, suicides, and homicides are the leading cause of death in young people 15 to 24 years of age. In many cases the deaths are directly related to drug use.

THE ENCYCLOPEDIA OF PSYCHOACTIVE DRUGS answers the questions that young people are likely to ask about drugs, as well as those they might not think to ask, but should. Topics include: what it means to be intoxicated; how drugs affect mood; why people take drugs; who takes them; when they take them; and how much they take. They will learn what happens to a drug when it enters the body. They will learn what it means to get "hooked" and how it happens. They will learn how drugs affect their driving, their schoolwork, and those around them—their peers, their family, their friends, and their employers. They will learn what the signs are that indicate that a friend or a family member may have a drug problem and to identify four stages leading from drug use to drug abuse. Myths about drugs are dispelled.

National surveys indicate that students are eager for information about drugs and that they respond to it. Students not only need information about drugs—they want information. How they get it often proves crucial. Providing young people with accurate knowledge about drugs is one of the most critical aspects.

THE ENCYCLOPEDIA OF PSYCHOACTIVE DRUGS synthesizes the wealth of new information in this field and demystifies this complex and important subject. Each volume in the series is written by an expert in the field. Handsomely illustrated, this multi-volume series is geared for teenage readers. Young people will read these books, share them, talk about them, and make more informed decisions because of them.

Miriam Cohen, Ph.D.
Contributing Editor

A Xanax tablet compressor. Alprazolam (trademarked Xanax), developed in 1969, appears to be more effective than Valium in treating depression, and causes fewer side effects, such as daytime drowsiness.

INTRODUCTION

The Gift of Wizardry
Use and Abuse

JACK H. MENDELSON, M.D.

NANCY K. MELLO, PH.D.

Alcohol and Drug Abuse Research Center
Harvard Medical School—McLean Hospital

Dorothy to the Wizard:

"I think you are a very bad man," said Dorothy.
"Oh, no, my dear; I'm really a very good man; but I'm a very bad Wizard."

—from THE WIZARD OF OZ

Man is endowed with the gift of wizardry, a talent for discovery and invention. The discovery and invention of substances that change the way we feel and behave are among man's special accomplishments, and like so many other products of our wizardry, these substances have the capacity to harm as well as to help. The substance itself is neutral, an intricate molecular structure. Yet, "too much" can be sickening, even deadly. It is man who decides how each substance is used, and it is man's beliefs and perceptions that give this neutral substance the attributes to heal or destroy.

Consider alcohol—available to all and yet regarded with intense ambivalence from biblical times to the present day. The use of alcoholic beverages dates back to our earliest ancestors. Alcohol use and misuse became associated with the worship of gods and demons. One of the most powerful Greek gods was Dionysus, lord of fruitfulness and god of wine. The Romans adopted Dionysus but changed his name to Bacchus. Festivals and holidays associated with Bacchus celebrated the harvest and the origins of life. Time has blurred the images of the Bacchanalian festival, but the theme of drunkenness as a major part of celebration has survived the pagan gods and remains a familiar part of modern society.

The term "Bacchanalian festival" conveys a more appealing image than "drunken orgy" or "pot party," but whatever the label, some of the celebrants will inevitably start up the "high" escalator to the next plateau. Once there, the de-escalation is difficult for many.

According to reliable estimates, one out of every ten Americans develops a serious alcohol-related problem sometime in his or her lifetime. In addition, automobile accidents caused by drunken drivers claim the lives of tens of thousands every year. Many of the victims are gifted young people, just starting out in adult life. Hospital emergency rooms abound with patients seeking help for alcohol-related injuries.

Who is to blame? Can we blame the many manufacturers who produce such an amazing variety of alcoholic beverages? Should we blame the educators who fail to explain the perils of intoxication, or so exaggerate the dangers of drinking that no one could possibly believe them? Are friends to blame— those peers who urge others to "drink more and faster," or the macho types who stress the importance of being able to "hold your liquor"? Casting blame, however, is hardly constructive, and pointing the finger is a fruitless way to deal with problems. Alcoholism and drug abuse have few culprits but many victims. Accountability begins with each of us, every time we choose to use or to misuse an intoxicating substance.

It is ironic that some of man's earliest medicines, derived from natural plant products, are used today to poison and to intoxicate. Relief from pain and suffering is one of society's many continuing goals. Over 3,000 years ago, the Therapeutic Papyrus of Thebes, one of our earliest written records, gave instructions for the use of opium in the treatment of pain. Opium, in the form of its major derivative, morphine, remains one of the most powerful drugs we have for pain relief. But opium, morphine, and similar compounds, such as heroin, have also been used by many to induce changes in mood and feeling. Another example of man's misuse of a natural substance is the coca leaf, which for centuries was used by the Indians of Peru to reduce fatigue and hunger. Its modern derivative, cocaine, has important medical use as a local anesthetic. Unfortunately, its increasing abuse in the 1980s has reached epidemic proportions.

The purpose of this series is to provide information about the nature and behavioral effects of alcohol and drugs, and the probable consequences of their use. The information presented here (and in other books in this series) is based on many clinical and laboratory studies and observations by people from diverse walks of life.

Over the centuries, novelists, poets, and dramatists have provided us with many insights into the beneficial and problematic aspects of alcohol and drug use. Physicians, lawyers, biologists, psychologists, and social scientists have contributed to a better understanding of the causes and consequences of using these substances. The authors in this series have attempted to gather and condense all the latest information about drug use and abuse. They have also described the sometimes wide gaps in our knowledge and have suggested some new ways to answer many difficult questions.

One such question, for example, is how do alcohol and drug problems get started? And what is the best way to treat them when they do? Not too many years ago, alcoholics and drug abusers were regarded as evil, immoral, or both. It is now recognized that these persons suffer from very complicated diseases involving complex biological, psychological, and social problems. To understand how the disease begins and progresses, it is necessary to understand the nature of the substance, the behavior and genetic makeup of the afflicted person, and the characteristics of the society or culture in which he lives.

The diagram below shows the interaction of these three factors. The arrows indicate that the substance not only affects the user personally, but the society as well. Society influences attitudes towards the substance, which in turn affect its availability. The substance's impact upon the society may support or discourage the use and abuse of that substance.

SUBSTANCE
(ALCOHOL OR DRUG)

PERSON ← → SOCIETY

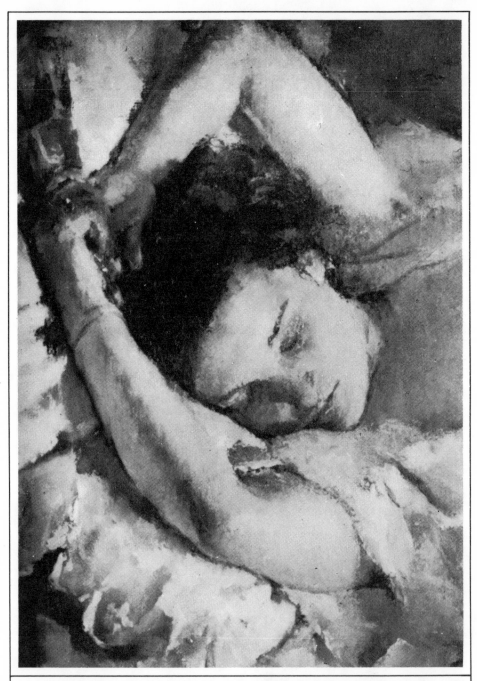

This painting by Giovanni Romagnoli, entitled "Riflesso di Sole" ("Reflection of the Sun"), depicts a woman in a deep sleep. An estimated 100 million Americans experience some form of insomnia, or difficulty in sleeping, during their lifetime.

Although many of the social environments we live in are very similar, some of the most subtle differences can strongly influence our thinking and behavior. Where we live, go to school and work, whom we discuss things with—all influence our opinions about drug use and misuse. Yet we also share certain commonly accepted beliefs that outweigh any differences in our attitudes. The authors in this series have tried to identify and discuss the central, most crucial issues concerning drug use and misuse.

Regrettably, man's wizardry in developing new substances in medical therapeutics has not always been paralleled by intelligent usage. Although we do know a great deal about the effects of alcohol and drugs, we have yet to learn how to impart that knowledge, especially to young adults.

Does it matter? What harm does it do to smoke a little pot or have a few beers? What is it like to be intoxicated? How long does it last? Will it make me feel really fine? Will it make me sick? What are the risks? These are but a few of the questions answered in this series, which, hopefully, will enable the reader to make wise decisions concerning the crucial issue of drugs.

Information sensibly acted upon can go a long way towards helping everyone develop his or her best self. As one keen and sensitive observer, Dr. Lewis Thomas, has said,

> *There is nothing at all absurd about the human condition. We matter. It seems to me a good guess, hazarded by a good many people who have thought about it, that we may be engaged in the formation of something like a mind for the life of this planet. If this is so, we are still at the most primitive stage, still fumbling with language and thinking, but infinitely capacitated for the future. Looked at this way, it is remarkable that we've come as far as we have in so short a period, really no time at all as geologists measure time. We are the newest, the youngest, and the brightest thing around.*

High school students gather to take exams in Nice, France. Anxiety, which stems from the anticipation of mental or emotional trauma, is often associated with a particular event, such as taking a test.

CHAPTER 1

ANXIETY AND THE MINOR TRANQUILIZERS

At one time or another, everyone has experienced anxiety—that unpleasant feeling of nervousness or apprehension about something that may or may not happen. Anxiety is frequently compared with fear. According to this analysis, fear is seen as being directed toward something specific, such as being stung by bumblebees, dying, or falling off a cliff, though the source of the anxiety is nonspecific. However, anxiety can be associated with a particular event, such as taking a test or being interviewed for a job. A more accurate distinction between fear and anxiety may be that fear is a concern about possible physical pain or personal danger, and anxiety is the result of the anticipation of possible emotional or mental trauma.

Normal anxiety can be beneficial. It is accompanied by physiological changes, including an increased output of the hormones epinephrine and norepinephrine, that heighten alertness. This, in turn, can help improve the functioning of the anxious person. For example, if a person is driving without a driver's license, anxiety about this may lead to more careful driving. And being anxious about passing a test will often contribute to a student's studying harder and longer.

On the other hand, anxiety is harmful if it interferes with a person's ability to respond appropriately to a situation. If a student is so worried about an upcoming examination that he or she cannot concentrate well enough to study, the anxiety is not helpful but is, in fact, disruptive. In addition, the anxiety that can result from an individual's inability to change the tension-producing situation may actually be dangerous. For example, a person who is told that he or she has a serious heart condition may become anxious, and this anxiety could make the condition worse.

When anxiety impairs a person's ability to cope with the problem that produces it, it may become necessary to try to reduce the distress. There are many ways to do this—the use of a minor tranquilizer, such as Valium, is only one possibility. This book will provide information about the advantages and disadvantages of taking Valium, as well as offer alternative strategies for dealing with anxiety.

In addition to "normal" anxiety—the kind many of us experience in a stressful situation—there are some kinds of anxiety that are so severe or long-lasting that they can be considered abnormal, or pathological. Psychiatrists divide pathological anxieties into two types: phobic disorders and anxiety states.

The two most common kinds of phobic disorder are simple phobias and agoraphobia. A simple phobia is an over-

A certain amount of anxiety can improve one's performance in stressful situations, such as a job interview. However, when anxiety becomes excessive it can disrupt a person's ability to cope with a given circumstance.

whelming fear of a specific class of objects or conditions, such as a fear of being closed in (claustrophobia), a fear of heights (acrophobia), or a fear of dirt or germs (mysophobia). Agoraphobia, which formally only referred to the fear of open spaces, is now considered to be a generalized fear of a wide variety of situations in which a person feels cut off from his or her point of security. It may be associated with a panic attack, in which, for example, a person is overwhelmed with a sudden fear of impending death. This type of attack is usually accompanied by severe physiological symptoms, including a rapid heartbeat, profuse sweating, and difficulty in breathing. A man who has had a panic attack in a grocery store may be afraid to return to that store. If he then has a panic attack in the park or the movie theater, these places will also become off-limits. In extreme cases, agoraphobiacs restrict themselves to their homes, the only place in which they feel safe from these attacks.

The other major type of pathological anxiety is the anxiety state, also called a generalized anxiety disorder. This condition is characterized by jitteriness, trembling, fatigue, and an inability to relax. A person suffering from this disorder

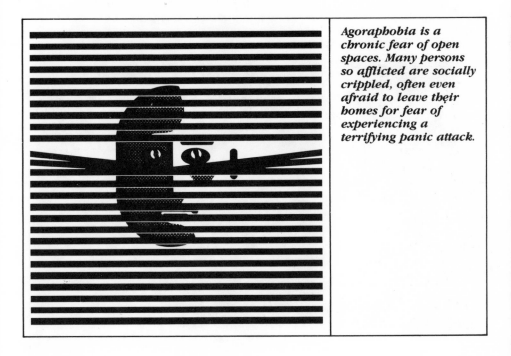

Agoraphobia is a chronic fear of open spaces. Many persons so afflicted are socially crippled, often even afraid to leave their homes for fear of experiencing a terrifying panic attack.

may experience a pounding or racing heart, heavy sweating, cold and clammy hands, an upset stomach, and increased frequency of urination. Other symptoms include irritability, sleep and concentration difficulties, and a constant fear that something bad is about to happen.

A generalized anxiety disorder is considered pathological, and therefore much more serious than everyday anxiety. Medical professionals discriminate between normal anxiety and generalized anxiety disorders in various ways. A generalized anxiety disorder is not usually a "situational" anxiety, meaning that it is not tied to a specific situation or condition. A person suffering from a generalized anxiety disorder is often unable to say what is producing the anxiety. If there is a specific concern, it may be more imaginary than real. Someone who constantly worries about having cancer when he or she exhibits no medical signs of the disease has an imaginary anxiety. Also, generalized anxiety disorders usually have a relatively long duration and frequently appear concurrently with other personality disturbances. In contrast, normal anxiety usually presents less severe symptoms, is commonly associated with a specific stressful situation, frequently develops in people who have no other personality disturbances, and usually does not last for long periods of time.

Physicians commonly prescribed barbiturates to treat anxiety before the discovery of minor tranquilizers, which proved safer and more effective, and had less potential for abuse, physical dependence, and overdose.

People suffering from pathological anxiety conditions—such as agoraphobia, panic attacks, or generalized anxiety disorders—are often in need of treatment, which usually involves the administration of drugs. People with normal anxiety are less likely to need treatment, though when they do they generally respond to treatments that do not involve drugs.

The optimum treatment for a pathological anxiety depends on the specific type of illness involved. The minor tranquilizers (anti-anxiety tranquilizers such as Valium, Librium, and Miltown) can be helpful in some cases. Other drugs and/or nondrug treatments are more useful in other cases. Even with anxiety problems that can be relieved by drugs, alternate methods can be helpful. In fact, many patients and physicians prefer nondrug treatment. A discussion of the appropriate use of Valium and other minor tranquilizers, as well as a consideration of different forms of therapy, is presented later.

Prior to the introduction of minor tranquilizers in the late 1950s, alcohol was the principal drug used to relieve anxiety. While drinking is still a popular and socially acceptable way to relax, the long-term problems that can result from frequent consumption overshadow any of alcohol's temporary beneficial effects.

Drugs for Anxiety: Alcohol and Barbiturates

Before the minor tranquilizers were introduced in the 1950s, other drugs were used to reduce anxiety. Alcohol, one of the oldest of these drugs, continues to be popular because it is readily available and socially acceptable—a person can drink alcohol without having to admit that he or she has an "anxiety problem." Though moderate amounts of alcohol may be reasonably effective in treating mild anxiety, few doctors would recommend its use, because there are serious physical and psychological difficulties associated with frequent overconsumption. It is not known whether people who drink alcohol to relieve anxiety drink more or are more likely to become alcoholics than people who drink for other reasons. However, studies have shown that alcohol consumption by alcoholics can actually lead to increased anxiety.

Barbiturates belong to a group of sedative drugs that depress the central nervous system and produce calmness, relaxation, and, in high doses, sleep. Before the discovery of safer and more effective drugs, they were widely prescribed for the relief of anxiety, and, to a limited extent, they are still used for this purpose. However, it is only within a very narrow range of doses that barbiturates and alcohol effectively

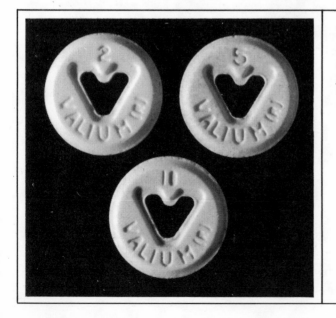

A new design for Valium reflects the drug industry's continuing search for products that are both appealing and identifiable.

reduce anxiety. If an individual ingests only a little more than the prescribed dose of either drug, the result is sleepiness or intoxication, both of which interfere with normal activity. Too small a dose will have little or no effect on anxiety.

Another undesirable characteristic of alcohol and the barbiturates is their tendency to produce tolerance and dependence. Tolerance is a physical and/or behavioral adaptation to a drug such that larger amounts are required to produce the original effects, or such that over time a fixed amount produces decreasing effects. If increasingly higher doses are ingested, there is a greater chance of suffering from dangerous side effects, including overdose or dependence.

Dependence develops when drugs such as alcohol or barbiturates have been used on a daily basis for a considerable period of time. As a result, the body adapts to the presence of the drug, such that its absence produces withdrawal symptoms. These may include tremors (extreme shakiness), hallucinations, and even convulsions.

Mixing tranquilizers with other drugs can result in a fatal overdose. The cause of Elvis Presley's death in 1977, originally attributed to a heart attack, was subsequently revealed as "polypharmacy," the lethal interaction of several drugs. Presley's physician reportedly wrote thousands of prescriptions, ranging from tranquilizers to narcotics, for Elvis during the singer's final two years.

Both alcohol and barbiturates have a high potential for abuse, which occurs when the drugs are taken more frequently than is medically necessary. This practice can cause behavioral, medical, and social impairment. Misuse of these drugs can also cause death. The barbiturates are particularly notorious because they have been used frequently as a means of committing suicide. The abuse of barbiturates can also produce confusion, which can lead to an accidental overdose and possibly death.

Miltown and Other Tranquilizers

The problems associated with alcohol and barbiturates seen in the 1940s made evident the need for a drug that would provide anti-anxiety effects at doses significantly lower than

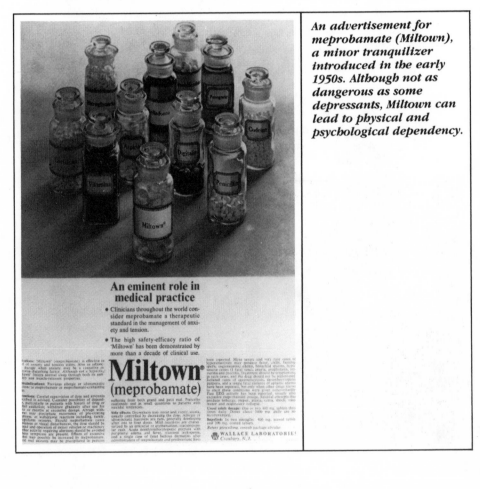

An advertisement for meprobamate (Miltown), a minor tranquilizer introduced in the early 1950s. Although not as dangerous as some depressants, Miltown can lead to physical and psychological dependency.

those that would produce intoxication or drowsiness. Such a drug would also be less likely to produce tolerance and dependence, would carry less risk of abuse, and would be much less likely to cause death if an overdose was intentionally or accidentally taken.

In the early 1950s researchers developed a drug that they felt would satisfy these criteria. This drug was called meprobamate (commonly known as Miltown), a member of a new class of drugs called "minor tranquilizers." Miltown, however, was soon found to create some of the same undesirable effects as the older sedatives. It produced dependence if taken regularly, and an overdose resulted in dangerous intoxication. Furthermore, meprobamate was as likely to be abused as the barbiturates. Although Miltown is still used today to treat anxiety, it has largely been replaced by drugs with fewer undesirable side effects.

Some of the drugs currently prescribed for anxiety are classified as antihistamines. These are very similar to the medicines used in some nonprescription cold and allergy remedies. The modest anti-anxiety effects of the antihistamines result from their ability to produce mild sedation. Since these effects are not strong, these drugs are probably most useful in cases of low-level anxiety.

Inderal (pictured here) belongs to a newer group of drugs called beta-blockers, and is primarily used to treat high blood pressure and irregular heartbeat. Without causing sedation, Inderal blocks the effects of the hormone norepinephrine, which is released in the body in stressful situations.

Beta-Blockers

A newer group of drugs currently being used to treat some types of anxiety are the beta-blockers (or propranolol, marketed under the trade name Inderal). Used primarily for the treatment of high blood pressure and irregular heartbeat, they act by blocking some of the effects of norepinephrine, a hormone released in large amounts by the body during periods of stress. Norepinephrine is in part responsible for the increased heart rate, shakiness, and stomach upset common in a stressful situation. The beta-blockers can reduce these effects, and they do not produce sedation. Beta-blockers may be particularly useful for people who are anxious about an upcoming, short-term event, such as making a speech or going for a job interview. These are situations where tremors, stomach upset, and drowsiness are especially unwelcome.

According to the National Prescription Audit, which measures prescriptions dispensed by retail pharmacies, Valium was the most popular minor tranquilizer in the United States from 1975–1980.

New Drugs for Anxiety

Today there is a large market for anti-anxiety drugs, and pharmaceutical companies invest heavily in the search for new substances that will relieve anxiety without producing dangerous side effects. One such drug, buspirone, has been available in Europe since the early 1980s. Preliminary research suggests that buspirone may be useful in treating cases of mild, infrequent anxiety. This drug does not produce sedation, impair the ability to drive, or interact with alcohol. In addition, it does not appear to produce dependence or have a high potential for abuse. Buspirone will probably become available in the United States fairly soon, and researchers in this country will then be able to evaluate its effectiveness.

Benzodiazepines

In 1955 Dr. Leo Sternbach, a chemist working for the Hoffman-LaRoche drug company, synthesized a drug he thought was in the chemical family called *quinazoline N-oxides*. The drug was initially ignored because at the time the company was more interested in other projects. But two years later, during a general laboratory cleanup, the drug was rediscovered. Because other drugs in the chemical family of the new substance had failed to prove useful, few researchers were optimistic about this one. However, further laboratory evaluation showed that the new drug produced effects that were very different from those of its related compounds. One of its most impressive attributes was its ability to calm laboratory animals. Following administration of this drug, even wild monkeys became much less aggressive and could be handled by the laboratory staff. In experimental animals the drug also produced muscle relaxation and prevented convulsions.

When the chemistry of the drug was further evaluated, it was found not to have the structure Dr. Sternbach originally thought it had. In fact, it was a benzodiazepine (a minor tranquilizer) and was given the name *chlordiazepoxide*. After extensive tests on animals, this drug was marketed under the trade name Librium and prescribed as a new treatment for anxiety that was either caused by stressful situations or had no clear cause.

29

In an attempt to determine what aspects of Librium's chemical structure were related to which aspects of its effects, several other drugs in the benzodiazepine family were synthesized by the researchers. Although most of them produced effects very similar to those of Librium, one was found to be much more potent. (This means that much less of the drug was required to produce the same effects.) This drug, which was given the generic name *diazepam* and the trade name Valium, was also put on the market as an effective treatment for anxiety.

In the 1960s and early 1970s, Valium and Librium seemed to meet nearly all the criteria for a good treatment of anxiety. They produced little sedation at effective doses, were quite safe even when taken in large amounts, and appeared to produce little risk of dependence or abuse. These two drugs became immensely popular, indicating that a great many people felt a need for such medication—or that their physicians believed they had such a need.

Since the development of Librium and Valium, hundreds of other benzodiazepines have been synthesized by drug companies. Eleven benzodiazepines are currently available by a

Most studies indicate that Valium is considerably effective in reducing anxiety in long-lasting disorders. However, Valium has not proven as successful in the treatment of phobias based on specific conditions, such as acrophobia, or the fear of heights.

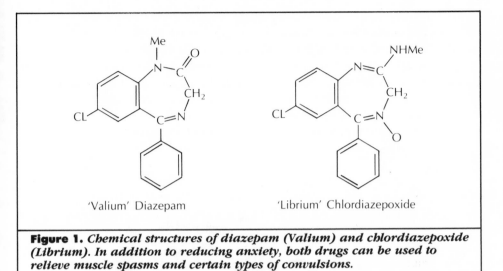

'Valium' Diazepam   'Librium' Chlordiazepoxide

Figure 1. *Chemical structures of diazepam (Valium) and chlordiazepoxide (Librium). In addition to reducing anxiety, both drugs can be used to relieve muscle spasms and certain types of convulsions.*

doctor's prescription in the United States, and an additional 13 are available in other countries. Several others now being tested in animals may eventually become available for human use. These drugs are used primarily for anxiety relief, although several of them are used as sleeping pills or hypnotics, and one is thought to be effective against depressions. Some of the drugs that are under investigation may prove useful in producing anesthesia (loss of sensation and/or loss of consciousness) for surgery.

Except in their potency (the dose required to produce an effect) and their duration of action, there is not a great deal of variety in the effects produced by most of the benzodiazepines. However, two of those available in the United States, alprazolam and clorazepate, have chemical actions that are different from the others. Clorazepate (trademarked Tranxene) is useful in the treatment of some seizure disorders, and alprazolam (trademarked Xanax) appears to be more effective against depression than other tranquilizers in this family.

The Effectiveness of the Minor Tranquilizers

It is essential for physicians to be sure that the drugs they prescribe will do what they are supposed to do. For example, how do the doctors know that the minor tranquilizers, for

Table 1

Benzodiazepines Available in the United States			
NAME	GENERIC NAME	USE	DURATION
Ativan	Lorazepam	Preanesthesia, Anxiety	Short
Centrax	Prazepam	Anxiety	Long
Dalmane	Flurazepam	Insomnia	Very Long
Halcion	Triazolam	Insomnia	Very Short
Librium	Chlordiazepoxide	Anxiety	Intermediate
Paxipam	Halazepam	Anxiety	Long
Restoril	Temazepam	Insomnia	Short
Serax	Oxazepam	Anxiety	Short
Tranxene	Clorazepate	Anxiety, Seizures	Long
Valium	Diazepam	Anxiety	Intermediate
Xanax	Alprazolam	Anxiety, Panic, Depression	Short

example, will really help relieve a person's anxiety? The best way to make a clinical evaluation of a drug is to use a technique called a *double-blind, placebo-controlled experiment*. A placebo is an inactive substance that looks exactly like the active substance being tested. Double blind means that neither the giver nor the receiver of the substance knows if what is being given is the active medication or the placebo. Until the experiment has been completed, this information is known only to a person who is not directly involved in measuring the drug's effects. This procedure ensures that both the researchers and the subjects are objective when it comes to evaluating the effects of the ingested substance. At the beginning of each double-blind experiment, the subjects are told that the substance they will receive may be the active medication or the placebo.

In a double-blind, placebo-controlled study of the effectiveness of minor tranquilizers, the subjects' initial levels of anxiety must be determined before any pills are given. This is often done by giving the participants a questionnaire that includes statements such as "I sometimes feel out of control," "My heart beats so hard it frightens me," and "I have trouble sleeping because I am so nervous." The subjects' responses can be evaluated to determine each individual's level of anxiety. After the researchers have estimated each participant's normal level of anxiety, they administer either the drug or a placebo for at least one week—frequently for much longer. Anxiety is measured again at the end of the drug-administration period, and a comparison between the two sets of data is made. If, after the experiment, those receiving the active drug are measurably less anxious than those receiving the placebo, the investigators have some evidence that the drug is effective.

In most such studies of the effects of Valium and its related compounds on anxiety, the results have indicated that the drugs are considerably more effective in reducing anxiety than a placebo. Several of these studies have indicated that some groups of people are helped more by benzodiazepines than others. For example, people with higher levels of anxiety appear to benefit from drug administration more than those with lower levels of anxiety.

The studies that have demonstrated the effectiveness of minor tranquilizers in treating anxiety have chiefly studied people who have fairly severe, long-lasting disorders. However, tranquilizers, particularly Valium, are used frequently

Most of the demands of daily living do not warrant taking tranquilizers. People who use drugs such as Valium simply to unwind or get to sleep run the risk of becoming addicted.

by people with less severe, relatively temporary anxiety that is brought on by specific stressful events. Unfortunately, medical studies have told us very little about the ability of Valium to relieve this type of anxiety. The double-blind, placebo-controlled studies have not indicated that minor tranquilizers reduce short-term, situational anxiety. This is not necessarily because they really do not work. It is more likely because the study lasts longer than the anxiety does. Thus, if two patients participate in a study in which one receives a placebo and the other receives Valium and their anxiety lasts for only three days, they may show no differences at the end of one week. This does not mean that the drug was not helpful or that there are not instances when it should be given for short-term anxiety. What this really means is that better studies need to be designed specifically to test the effectiveness of minor tranquilizers for this purpose.

Even though experimental studies indicate that minor tranquilizers are effective in treating long-term anxiety and have not yet demonstrated a clear effect on short-term anx-

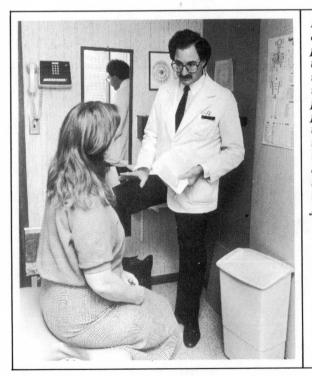

Physicians should exercise great caution in prescribing minor tranquilizers, carefully monitoring their use and making certain the patient receives psychological counseling to supplement the medication. Unfortunately, many doctors are all too willing to prescribe drugs just to make their patients feel a little better.

iety, some reputable psychiatrists may recommend these drugs for short-term anxiety and suggest nondrug treatment for long-term anxiety. This is not as irrational as it may first appear. Physicians who have given tranquilizers for a few days to patients with short-term, situation-induced anxiety have often observed improvement, even if experimental studies have not demonstrated such a benefit. But tranquilizers given over the course of months or years can produce some problems (see Chapter 3). Thus, when a person appears to have chronic, or long-term, anxiety, it may be better to avoid prolonged use of these drugs and search for another treatment.

The Controversy over the Benzodiazepines

If Valium and other benzodiazepines are so successful in the treatment of anxiety, why has there been so much concern about their use? One of the major reasons is that Valium is used to treat anxiety, which is a condition occasionally experienced by everyone. When more prescriptions are written for a certain drug than for almost any other drug and when that drug is used to treat a "normal" condition, there is reason to be concerned. Is a large portion of the population needlessly and harmfully placing a chemical barrier between itself and the stresses and strains of life? Are physicians and drug companies encouraging the use of this chemical barrier because it makes patients' lives temporarily easier, or because it greatly increases their own incomes? Some abuses are almost certainly occurring, but these cases seem to be in the minority.

To decide whether or not a particular individual should be given Valium or a related medication, the most important questions to ask are: Will it help the person adjust to or get through the anxiety-producing situation? Is he or she better able to function as a result of taking the drug? Does the drug make life less painful for a person subjected to a stressful condition that cannot be altered? If the answer to all these questions is yes, then in that situation and for that individual the use of the drug may be appropriate. If use of the benzodiazepine impedes a person's ability to deal with a situation, if he or she would prefer to confront the particular burden rather than seek temporary relief with a pill, or if the drug produces undesirable or dangerous side effects in the individual, then it is certainly inadvisable for the benzodiazepine to be administered.

A woman who is abused by her husband but is afraid to leave him because she has no job or skills of her own may suffer from anxiety severe enough to warrant anti-anxiety medication. Should Valium be prescribed? It depends. Clearly, both the woman and her husband need counseling that will either lead to a change in their relationship or help her gain the strength to face a change in her life. If Valium can reduce her anxiety to a level at which she is capable of making appropriate and rational decisions about her life, then it makes sense to use the medication. But if she uses Valium as a crutch or takes it in high doses in order to escape the reality of the situation, then taking the drug is not appropriate. Of course, if a physician considers the patient's problem serious enough to warrant a prescription for Valium, the doctor should also consider it his or her responsibility to counsel the patient about the problem or to refer the patient to someone who can provide proper psychological assistance.

An estimated 2% to 5% of the U.S. population suffers from panic attacks, unpredictable bouts of extreme irrational terror. The effects of Valium on severe short-term anxiety have yet to be determined.

Tranquilizers should rarely be prescribed as the only treatment for an anxiety condition. At the very least, frequent follow-up contact with the patient is required. The questions that must be repeatedly asked are: Is the drug helping? Is the dose still appropriate? Is the drug's continued use necessary? Both physician and patient must exercise responsibility when they are dealing with anti-anxiety medication. The doctor who regards Valium as an innocuous remedy that can be safely prescribed and represcribed is making a serious error. The patient who fails to pay close attention to whether or not the drug is helping, or whether the situation continues to warrant medication is also running a risk. The minor tranquilizers are powerful medicines. As well as having benefits, they can have serious side effects. Both doctor and patient need to be aware of these potential dangers, and need to be cautious in prescribing and using these drugs.

Help for Other Types of Anxiety

There are many types of anxiety. Not all of them should or can be treated in the same way. Panic attacks, in which the anxiety is so severe that the sufferer believes he or she is going to die and which can result in agoraphobia, are debilitating but treatable. For reasons that no one yet understands, panic attacks and agoraphobia are not effectively treated by the more common anti-anxiety medicines. However, such attacks can frequently be reduced by drugs that are effective in treating depression. One of the benzodiazepines, alprazolam (Xanax), appears to be helpful in the treatment of panic attacks. Interestingly, it is the only benzodiazepine used to treat depression. The fact that this drug can help to relieve both conditions suggests a connection between depression and panic attacks. Although people who are depressed do not appear to be prone to panic attacks, it is possible that similar alterations in the biochemistry of the brain lead to panic attacks in some people and depression in others. Drugs that correct or modify these alterations— either Xanax or the tricyclic antidepressants, such as amitriptyline (Elavil)—are helpful in treating both panic attacks and depression.

If they become incapacitating, phobias are probably best treated with behavioral therapy. Phobias are usually thought

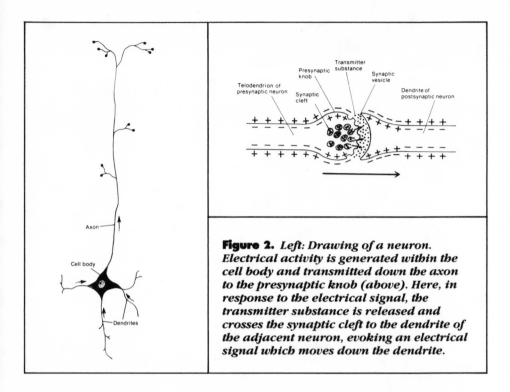

Figure 2. *Left: Drawing of a neuron. Electrical activity is generated within the cell body and transmitted down the axon to the presynaptic knob (above). Here, in response to the electrical signal, the transmitter substance is released and crosses the synaptic cleft to the dendrite of the adjacent neuron, evoking an electrical signal which moves down the dendrite.*

to be due to a connection between a specific situation or object (such as heights, dogs, or flying) and a terrifying experience. In behavioral therapy, the sufferer is gradually desensitized to the cause of the fear by gradually being exposed to it in a supportive atmosphere where relaxation is encouraged. For example, a person with a phobia about dogs may be given a stuffed dog to start with, then a real puppy, then a small dog, and finally a larger, adult animal. At each step, the person is encouraged to interact with the dog and to practice prescribed relaxation procedures if anxiety develops. The administration of drugs is usually unnecessary.

How the Benzodiazepines Work

The nerves of the body and the brain communicate with each other primarily through chemical compounds called *neurotransmitters*. The neurotransmitters, which are released from the axon, or end, of one activated nerve, pass across a *synapse*, or narrow gap, to activate the *dendrite*, or receiving nerve ending, of the next nerve. This nerve, in turn, transmits a neurotransmitter to the next nerve, and so on. Each dendrite contains many small areas called *receptors*, which are sensitive to the neurotransmitter released by the sending nerve. It is believed that drugs affect the body by acting on the same receptors that are sensitive to the neurotransmitter. Because of its resemblance to a neurotransmitter, a drug may interact with the receptors and cause the nerves to respond as though they were being activated by the sending nerves and their neurotransmitters. Drugs may also modify the ability of nerves to send or receive their neurotransmitters by acting on receptors or by directly changing the structure of the membrane that surrounds the nerve.

Research focusing on benzodiazepines has found that these drugs bind (attach) to specific receptors, which have been named the benzodiazepine receptors. All of the many benzodiazepines that have been shown to be capable of reducing anxiety have also proved capable of binding to the

In behavior therapy, which appears to be more effective than drugs in treating many phobias, one is gradually exposed to the feared situation until he or she is "desensitized" to the cause of the fear.

benzodiazepine receptors. Furthermore, the more effective a benzodiazepine is in relieving anxiety, the more strongly it binds to the receptors. This suggests that the ability of the benzodiazepines to bind to their receptors is directly related to their ability to reduce anxiety. Other drugs that are capable of reducing anxiety, such as meprobamate (Miltown), the barbiturates, and alcohol, do not bind to the benzodiazepine receptors. These receptors, then, rather than being generally related to anxiety reduction, are specific to a particular anxiety medication—the benzodiazepines.

Of course, the human body did not evolve with benzodiazepine receptors in anticipation of Leo Sternbach's synthesis of the benzodiazepines. Scientists believe that the body may manufacture some material that acts on what scientists have labeled the benzodiazepine receptors to lower anxiety. Hoping to discover a natural anxiety-reducing substance, scientists are trying to isolate and identify this hypothetical material.

Scientists do not yet fully understand what happens after benzodiazepines bind to receptors, but at least part of the story has been uncovered. A neurotransmitter called gamma-aminobutyric acid (GABA), which is found in the brain and the spinal cord, acts to reduce the activity of the nerves that it contacts. GABA does not bind to the benzodiazepine receptors, but it is able to increase the receptor-binding activity of the benzodiazepines. (GABA is specific to the benzodiazepine receptor and thus does not increase the binding of other drugs to their receptors.) Benzodiazepines, in turn, are able to increase the binding of GABA to its own receptor. The reciprocal enhancement of receptor binding by these two compounds leads scientists to believe that the benzodiazepine receptor is structurally similar to the GABA receptor. They theorize that the benzodiazepines work by enhancing GABA's ability to decrease the activity of many groups of nerves in the brain and the spinal cord.

This information about where the benzodiazepines may act in the body does little to explain why these drugs have anti-anxiety, anti-epileptic, and muscle-relaxing effects. However, scientists have developed some theories about these interactions. According to some researchers, anxiety is a state that is created by an anatomical and biochemical circuit in the brain called the limbic system. It is a very old area of the

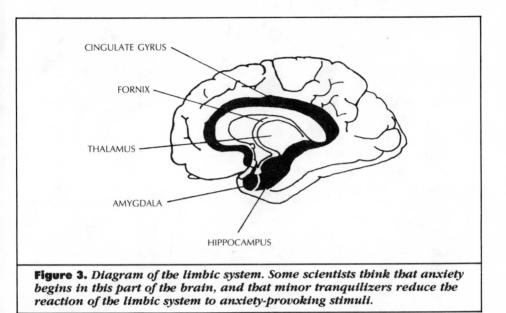

Figure 3. *Diagram of the limbic system. Some scientists think that anxiety begins in this part of the brain, and that minor tranquilizers reduce the reaction of the limbic system to anxiety-provoking stimuli.*

brain that is present in evolutionarily simple animals as well as in the more recently developed "higher" animals, such as humans.

Researchers have found that damage in certain parts of the limbic system can result in changes in emotional behavior. Monkeys that normally display fear and aggression toward humans have been shown to become quite tame when specific areas of their limbic systems are destroyed. In rats, the stimulation of other areas of this system with a very mild electrical current, applied so as to imitate activated nerves, produces reactions of defensiveness and fear.

Scientists speculate that the benzodiazepines enhance the inhibitory effects of GABA within the limbic system, thus reducing the reaction of this system to anxiety-provoking events. At the same time, the benzodiazepines may reduce the ability of other neurotransmitters to stimulate a fear reaction.

The complex actions of the benzodiazepines are still beyond our understanding, as is the complexity of the human emotional system, but these theories suggest the picture that may emerge when scientists have finally deciphered all the clues in the benzodiazepine mystery.

Painting by Johann Fussli entitled "The Nightmare." Minor tranquilizers are safer and more effective over a longer period of time than are barbiturates in relieving sleep disorders such as insomnia.

CHAPTER 2

BEYOND ANXIETY: THE MANY USES OF BENZODIAZEPINES

Because they produce sedation, relax muscles, and relieve anxiety, the benzodiazepines are very effective in relieving sleep disorders such as insomnia—difficulty in falling or staying asleep. Like anxiety, insomnia can be a "normal" part of life. Almost everybody experiences it at one time or another, but some people suffer more frequently from sleep problems—or from the fear of them—than others. Using drugs to combat insomnia has many of the same drawbacks as using them to treat anxiety, although this has not received as much negative publicity.

Barbiturates were once commonly prescribed for insomnia, but they have been largely displaced by the benzodiazepines, which are effective in promoting and maintaining sleep without causing some of the barbiturates' more serious side effects. For example, it is much more difficult to overdose with the benzodiazepines. A person who tries to commit suicide by consuming a high dose of sleeping pills, or a person who becomes confused after taking some sleeping medication and accidentally takes more, will be in much less danger if the drug is a benzodiazepine than if it is a barbiturate.

Barbiturates also have the capacity to increase the rate at which they are metabolized. This means that barbiturates, if they have been taken over a long period, will be broken down by the body with increasing speed and will have a much shorter duration of action. Therefore, they will become less effective in maintaining sleep and may even produce insomnia. The patient, unaware that much of his or her sleeping problem is being caused by the sleeping pills themselves, may increase the dosage, still sleep quite poorly, and risk an overdose. Since the benzodiazepines do not increase the rate of their own metabolism, they are therefore less likely to lose effectiveness with long-term administration.

The Treatment of Withdrawal from Alcohol and Barbiturates

Benzodiazepines are extremely helpful in the treatment of severe cases of alcohol and barbiturate withdrawal. Withdrawal occurs when large doses of the drug have been consumed for a period of several weeks or months and then are suddenly discontinued. Withdrawal symptoms usually start with muscle tremors and profuse sweating. As time passes, the sufferer may experience hallucinations, such as seeing spots or "pink elephants." If the drug dosage has been large enough and has been continued over a long period, the user may develop convulsions after the hallucinations. The most severe alcohol withdrawal symptom is delirium tremens, or the DTs, which may occur several days after the convulsive episodes have stopped. During the DTs, hallucinations reap-

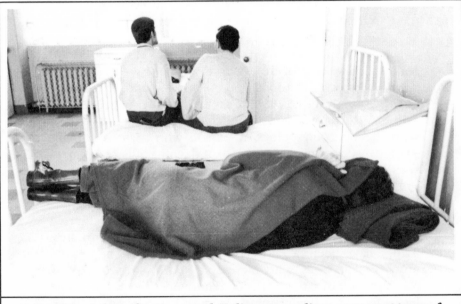

Patients in a detoxification ward. Valium can relieve some symptoms of alcohol and barbiturate withdrawal, including delirium tremens (DTs).

pear, but they are much more frightening and realistic. The person's temperature rises, and he or she becomes extremely agitated. If the body's system for controlling blood pressure is sufficiently disrupted, the DTs may cause death.

The most appropriate action on the part of the physician who is treating someone in alcohol or barbiturate withdrawal is to give the patient an injection of Valium or Librium. This medication will quickly stop any convulsions, tremors, and sweating. The benzodiazepines will also prevent the DTs associated with alcohol withdrawal if they are given before the person reaches this stage. However, it is not entirely certain that Valium or Librium will eliminate the DTs once they have started.

Why are the benzodiazepines so effective in treating withdrawal from alcohol and barbiturates? After long exposure to these drugs, the body's processes become dependent on them for proper functioning and are disrupted when the drugs are abruptly removed. The effects of withdrawal can be reversed by simply taking more of the drug that caused the problem in the first place: alcohol or barbiturates. Because benzodiazepines have many effects in common with these two drugs, they can be substituted for them in the individual who is undergoing withdrawal. The body will re-

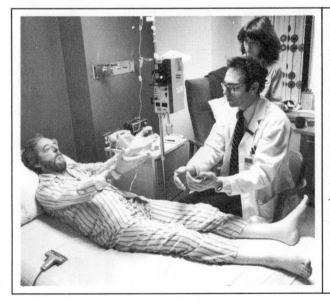

A patient undergoing treatment for multiple sclerosis, a painful neuromuscular disease affecting the spinal cord and brain. High doses of Valium can make a patient more comfortable by relaxing muscle spasms resulting from spinal cord damage. However, such doses can also produce sedative side effects that may limit a patient's ability to function.

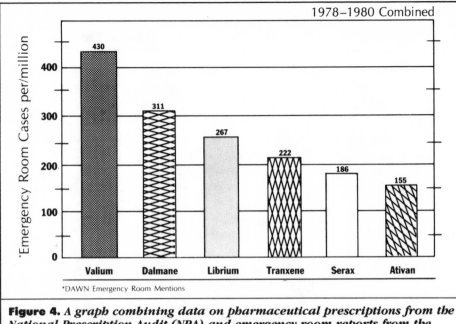

Figure 4. *A graph combining data on pharmaceutical prescriptions from the National Prescription Audit (NPA) and emergency room reports from the Drug Abuse Warning Network (DAWN). During a three-year period, an average of 430 people were admitted to emergency rooms for Valium abuse per every million prescriptions for the drug.*

spond as if it has received the drug on which it is dependent.

Benzodiazepines are better for the treatment of withdrawal than alcohol or barbiturates primarily because they are much safer and longer lasting. A relatively wide range of doses of Valium or Librium can be given to a person in alcohol or barbiturate withdrawal without producing oversedation or depressed rates of breathing. It would be difficult to give exactly enough alcohol or barbiturate to stop withdrawal signs without risking an overdose.

Treatment of withdrawal consists of relieving the symptoms quickly and then preventing their recurrence by slowly reducing the amount of drug in the body. Valium acts rapidly to relieve the withdrawal symptoms and, because it is excreted from the body slowly, gives the body time to get used to functioning without the alcohol or the barbiturate. Administering gradually smaller doses of Valium several times a day is one of the best ways to treat alcohol or barbiturate withdrawal signs.

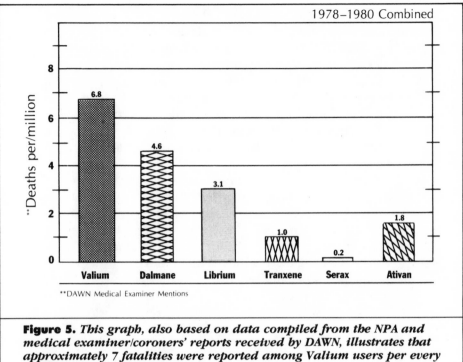

Figure 5. *This graph, also based on data compiled from the NPA and medical examiner/coroners' reports received by DAWN, illustrates that approximately 7 fatalities were reported among Valium users per every million prescriptions for the drug.*

Treatment of Muscle Spasms and Neuromuscular Disorders

One of the effects produced by the benzodiazepines is muscle relaxation. Tightly contracted muscles may result from strychnine poisoning, infections (such as tetanus), spinal cord damage (such as that occurring with cerebral palsy or multiple sclerosis), or simple muscle strain. It is necessary to relax these muscles, and Valium can be helpful or even lifesaving.

Strychnine is the active ingredient in some rat poisons. If ingested accidentally, it can produce severe muscle spasms, convulsions, and a contraction of the muscles associated with respiration that leads to death due to a lack of oxygen. Because Valium relaxes muscles, it can effectively relieve these symptoms.

Tetanus occurs when a wound is infected with bacteria that produce a toxin (poison) that causes severe muscle rigidity. In the most serious cases, the muscles of virtually the entire body are affected and convulsions may occur. Tetanus is often fatal, but the use of Valium, which relaxes the rigid muscles and acts as an anticonvulsant, has reduced the mortality rate. The anti-anxiety effects of Valium are also helpful in tetanus cases, since the victim, who remains conscious during the course of the disease, is under severe psychological as well as physical stress. This may be why one of the common problems associated with tetanus is bleeding from gastric ulcers.

Massive doses of Valium are used in treating tetanus, and steady monitoring of the dosage is required to ensure muscle relaxation without excessive depression of other bodily functions. Since the high doses must be given for periods of three weeks or more, care must also be exercised when the medication is reduced. As the next chapter explains, a person given high doses of a benzodiazepine for long periods of time can become dependent on the drug, so withdrawal of the medication must be carried out with extreme caution.

Cerebral palsy and multiple sclerosis are two neuromuscular disorders (disorders involving the nerves and muscles). They are characterized by muscle contractions caused

Palsy victim Hunter Van Pelt plunges into the Pacific Ocean after bicycling across America. There is evidence that Valium reduces muscle problems and improves coordination in children with cerebral palsy.

by irreparable brain damage or progressive nerve disease. For these disorders Valium is less effective. There is as yet no cure for these diseases, and therefore the best that can be done is to administer drugs that will make the patient as functional and as comfortable as possible. Although some reports on the effects of Valium on children with cerebral palsy claim that the drug reduces muscle problems and improves coordination in about 50% of the patients who receive it, other studies indicate that Valium has no significant effect. Though these inconclusive results suggest that benzodiazepines are not particularly helpful in cases of cerebral palsy, the possibility that these drugs can help a few patients may make it worth trying them for short periods.

People with increased muscle tension and muscle spasm due to multiple sclerosis or spinal cord injury can be helped with Valium. However, the doses needed are high enough to produce drowsiness. Since these muscle problems are very likely to persist throughout the patient's life and can cause severe limitations in movement, the decision about whether to use Valium is one that only the patient can make. If the drug increases the patient's comfort and the amount of drowsiness produced is acceptable, it is reasonable to administer it. On the other hand, if the patient finds the sedative side effects too unpleasant, then clearly it is not advisable to prescribe the drug.

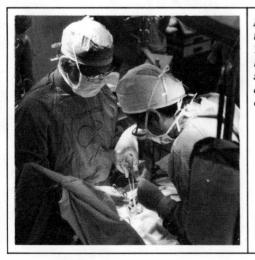

Minor tranquilizers are often given to patients before an operation. The drugs relax the patient, ease his or her concern about the surgery, and make the administration of anesthesia easier and more comfortable.

Another use of Valium—probably more widespread than it ought to be—is for relief of the muscle pain, spasm, and strain that sometimes follow injury. These problems can usually be treated effectively and safely with aspirin, application of local heat to the affected area, and appropriate exercise. However, if the spasm and pain are severe, Valium can be helpful. Certainly the drug should not be used alone but in conjunction with other therapies, and only on a short-term basis.

Treatment of Seizure Disorders

Valium is an excellent treatment for a particularly dangerous seizure condition called *status epilepticus*—an epileptic seizure that does not stop. The victim may have one seizure after another without gaining consciousness, and can suffer permanent brain damage or even die from a prolonged convulsion. When given intravenously (by injection into a vein), Valium quickly stops the seizures, and it is the drug of choice for these particularly dangerous convulsions. Valium is not used to treat other more common seizure disorders, how-

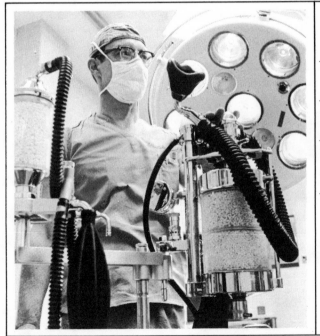

Valium and Librium are frequently combined with painkillers such as morphine or Demerol in moderate doses prior to surgery. Although Valium and Librium do not relieve pain, they do work with the painkillers to sedate the patient and reduce postoperative nausea.

ever, except those associated with alcohol or barbiturate withdrawal. Grand mal epilepsy, petit mal epilepsy, and other epileptic disorders are generally treated more effectively with medications that are not in the benzodiazepine family. But one benzodiazepine, clorazepate (Tranxene), is used along with other antiseizure drugs to treat some kinds of epilepsy.

Pre-operative Anesthesia

Benzodiazepines are frequently given to people prior to the administration of general anesthetics for surgical procedures. These drugs help relax the patient and reduce concern about the surgery. Sometimes they are given the night before surgery to help the patient sleep. Some people have criticized this practice, feeling that physicians could reduce presurgical anxiety without medication by taking the time to discuss the surgery with the patient. While it is certainly the responsibility of the surgeon and the anesthesiologist to explain the surgical procedures as thoroughly as possible, in most cases such explanations will not completely eliminate anxiety about the potential pain or undesirable consequences of the surgery. Anxiety does more harm than good in a situation like this, and it increases the discomfort of the patient considerably. Therefore, many doctors favor the use of presurgical tranquilizers.

Valium and Librium are often combined with narcotic analgesics (painkillers such as morphine or Demerol) and anticholinergic drugs (which decrease salivation and reduce potential complications in the administration of anesthetics that are inhaled). This combination of drugs is usually given before the patient is taken to the operating room. The narcotic analgesic—in addition to preventing or reducing the sensation of pain—sedates the patient and also produces some tranquilization. The Valium also tranquilizes the patient and makes the administration of anesthesia easier and less uncomfortable. While narcotics alone can provide some relief from anxiety, they are not as effective as Valium and may cause vomiting in the postoperative period. Valium alone, however, does not provide pain relief. Thus, the two kinds of drugs are used together in moderate doses to ease preoperative discomfort by providing relaxation, reducing anxiety, and decreasing responsiveness to pain.

In the film version of Barbara Gordon's book, I'm Dancing as Fast as I Can, *Jill Clayburgh dramatized the author's withdrawal from Valium. The book alerted the public to the potential for Valium dependency.*

CHAPTER 3

HOW DANGEROUS ARE THE MINOR TRANQUILIZERS?

*I*ngesting excessive doses of any drug can be dangerous. Even water can be fatal if many gallons of it are drunk over a period of a few hours. Since drugs can powerfully alter the body's functions, the concern must be not only with the dangers of taking excess amounts but also with the risks of taking the amount the doctor prescribes. The minor tranquilizers can be dangerous even when "taken as directed." Some of these dangers are related to the way the body reacts to their presence and the physical and behavioral changes that can occur following their ingestion. Other problems can develop in people who take Valium or Librium for relatively long periods and then abruptly stop taking the drug. This chapter will look at some of the findings from studies on the effects of both "normal" doses and overdoses of Valium. It will also examine some of the effects of combining Valium and alcohol.

Overdosing on Valium

When most people ask whether a drug is dangerous, they are interested in its immediate effects: "If I take 10 mg (milligrams) or 100 mg, will anything terrible happen to me in the next few minutes, hours, or days?" In this respect, the benzodiazepines are not very dangerous. If taken alone in a single dose, neither Valium nor any one of the other benzodiazepines will readily cause death. The literature on the effects of these tranquilizers reports only three or four cases in which a person died from taking an overdose of benzodiazepines.

Considering the vast number of such pills that have been taken and the very large number of people who have taken them, this speaks well for the safety of these drugs, at least with respect to overdosing on a single occasion.

Although people who overdose on Valium alone are not likely to die, they will, of course, have some problems, many of which are related to the drug's long duration of action. They may become unconscious, or at least be very difficult to rouse. They may sleep for a day or two and then be groggy and sedated for several more days. Their speech is likely to be slow and slurred, and walking may be difficult. They will feel and look as though they were drunk, though this Valium-produced condition will last longer than the drunkenness caused by alcohol.

The amount of Valium required to produce long-term sedation, grogginess, and even coma differs for each person. The reason for this is that the strength of the drug's effects depends upon many factors, including an individual's sensitivity to the drug and his or her body weight and size. On the average, however, a dose of 500 mg to 1000 mg will produce these effects. The therapeutic dose of Valium most

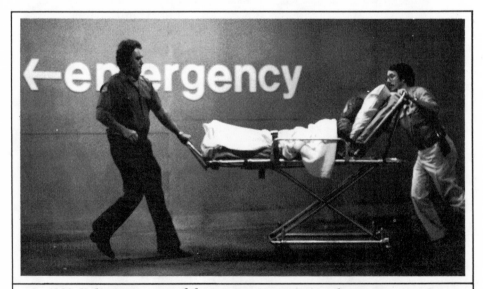

In 1980, Valium was one of the top two prescription drugs associated with emergency room admissions. The majority of abuse-related fatalities resulted from the combination of Valium and other drugs.

frequently prescribed by physicians for the treatment of anxiety is 2 mg to 10 mg, taken every 6 to 12 hours. However, even this dose can produce sedation and sleepiness, particularly in individuals who are not accustomed to the drug. Thus, it is not surprising that multiplying the therapeutic dose by 100 may lead to a more severe and long-lasting sedation. This is in contrast to the barbiturates, in which case merely doubling or tripling the therapeutic dose can lead to a life-threatening level of sedation.

Dangers of Long-Term Valium Use

There is more reason to be concerned about the dangers of long-term use of Valium than about the dangers of a one-time ingestion of the drug. The potential problems of Valium use were brought to the public's attention when television reported on the serious difficulty encountered by some people who had tried to stop taking the drug after using it for long periods. Further concern was created by the 1979 publication of Barbara Gordon's book, *I'm Dancing as Fast as I Can*, which documented the development of the author's severe thought disorders following termination of extended Valium use. One of the most serious problems highlighted by television and the book was the extreme ease with which Valium could be obtained. In one case, a physician recommended that his patient continue to take the drug despite her strong and justified feeling that it was harming her.

Because Valium use was so widespread at the time, these reports produced some public alarm. A great many Valium users and their families suddenly learned that this medicine was more dangerous than they had been led to believe. Many physicians were also worried by the evidence of Valium's potential dangers. They, too, had believed it to be a safe and effective drug, and now it appeared that even they had not been properly informed about its hazards. This concern was probably largely responsible for the decrease in Valium prescriptions that has occurred since the media headlined the drug's potential problems.

Though the information presented to the public may be factual, it is important to realize that the reported responses to Valium termination are probably unusually severe and perhaps (as in the case of the author of *I'm Dancing as Fast as I Can*) very uncommon. It is equally important to be aware of the more typical Valium withdrawal reaction. One needs to know why these particular people suffered as they did, what conditions may lead to a withdrawal reaction, how this reaction can be prevented, how it can be treated, and what potential withdrawal problems mean to the person whose anxiety, insomnia, or other problems are helped by the medication.

The experiences described as Valium withdrawal reactions are not reactions to the *presence* of Valium in the body. They are reactions to the *absence* of Valium, usually following long-term use of high doses of this drug. These reactions—most frequently jitteriness, tremors, anxiety, insomnia, strange tastes and smells, and under extreme conditions, convulsions—indicate physical dependence on the drug. Since use of the word "dependence" in connection with a drug as popular as Valium can alarm those who are taking the drug, it may be wise to examine this general phenomenon.

Physical dependence is a reaction of the body to the presence of substantial amounts of a drug over a long period of time. When the drug is no longer present, the body reacts and exhibits the disturbing symptoms known as drug with-

helium balloons.

valium balloons.

Abuse of Valium does not produce a "high." Exceeding the recommended dose of Valium most commonly produces grogginess and lethargy, as well as slurring of speech, tremor, stupor, and even coma.

Table 2

Demographics of Benzodiazepine Users and Abusers (1980)						
All Users*			Emergency Room Cases**			
Age	0–19	2%	Age	0–19	12%
	20–39	31%		20–39	62%
	40–59	36%		40–59	21%
	60+	31%		60+	4%
Sex	Male	36%	Sex	Male	36%
	Female	64%		Female	64%

* As reported by the National Disease and Therapeutic Index
** As reported by the Drug Abuse Warning Network (DAWN), which records the causes of emergency visits to 622 cooperating hospitals

drawal signs. Dependence is not related to self-control or to physical or psychological weakness. Dependence can be easily produced in experimental animals or even in tissues taken from experimental animals. It can even develop in the fetuses of women who have been exposed to sufficient amounts of certain drugs during pregnancy. Withdrawal signs can be quickly relieved by the administration of more of the drug that produced the dependence or by administration of other drugs from the same or similar drug class. Symptoms of withdrawal from one drug cannot be relieved by the administration of a drug that has a markedly different action on the body. For example, narcotic withdrawal cannot be treated with alcohol, or vice versa.

A person can develop dependence on a wide range of drugs that affect mental and emotional states, but narcotics (drugs that relieve pain) are notorious for producing dependence. People who have taken high doses of a narcotic for long periods and then abruptly stopped show signs resembling those that accompany a severe case of the flu. Their entire body aches, and they experience nausea, stomachaches, a runny nose, and tearing eyes. In addition, people who have been self-administering the drug and are aware that the same narcotic can relieve the withdrawal symptoms will have a strong craving for the drug.

Physical dependence on drugs from other classes is quite different from the dependence that develops with narcotics.

Withdrawal symptoms in people who are dependent on alcohol and barbiturates start with the tremors and jitteriness described earlier. Hallucinations, convulsions, and, in the most severe cases, delirium tremens can also occur during withdrawal from long-term intake of high doses of these drugs Researchers are not yet sure whether withdrawal from alcohol and barbiturates leads to the craving and drug-seeking behavior that characterizes cases of narcotics withdrawal. (Drug-seeking behavior is defined as an excessive involvement in obtaining and taking the drug.) In the case of other drugs, such as those used to treat schizophrenia or depression, physical dependence can develop, but withdrawal symptoms are quite unlike those described for narcotics or alcohol, and there is apparently no craving for the drugs during withdrawal.

The people whose cases were described on television were clearly suffering from Valium withdrawal. They had become dependent on the drug because they had taken high or very high doses of it for several months or years. And when they stopped taking the drug, they experienced the withdrawal symptoms characteristic of benzodiazepine withdrawal.

Benzodiazepine dependence was first demonstrated among mental-hospital patients who, in the 1960s, had been given very high doses of Librium for three to six months.

Even under a doctor's supervision, physical dependence can develop with long-term tranquilizer use. In 1978, after 14 years of taking minor tranquilizers prescribed by doctors to ease the pain of her arthritis and to help her sleep, former First Lady Betty Ford entered a treatment program to overcome her dependence on these drugs as well as alcohol.

When their medication was suddenly stopped, many of these patients developed withdrawal signs. It has recently become evident that dependence on benzodiazepines can even develop in people who take the relatively small doses that have been prescribed by their doctors. It is not yet clear why some people become dependent on therapeutic doses of Valium and others do not, although there are some indications that those who have had a pattern of drinking large amounts of alcohol may be more susceptible. What is clear is that both physicians and their patients must be aware that dependence on Valium can occur and that it should be avoided.

The literature about dependence on therapeutic doses of benzodiazepines indicates that many drug-dependent people seek out their doctors because they are having difficulty reducing or stopping their drug intake. When they try to change their drug intake, they report many of the withdrawal symptoms noted above. It is important to note that there is no evidence that these people are taking increasing amounts of their medication, lying to their doctors about their symptoms, or trying to convince their pharmacists to refill their prescriptions without their physician's authorization. In other words, dependence on tranquilizers does not

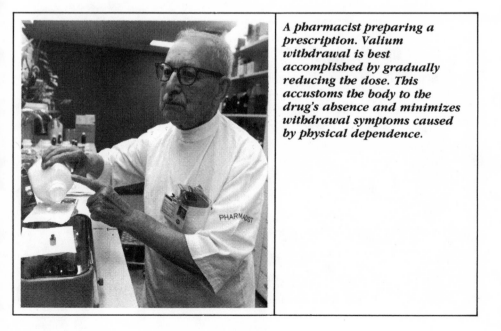

A pharmacist preparing a prescription. Valium withdrawal is best accomplished by gradually reducing the dose. This accustoms the body to the drug's absence and minimizes withdrawal symptoms caused by physical dependence.

often seem to produce a craving for, or abuse of, the drugs. It appears more likely that such patients seek help because they are concerned about the reactions they experience when they stop taking the drugs.

Fortunately, there is a safe and fairly easy way for a dependent person to stop taking Valium. Just as with alcohol or barbiturate withdrawal, the object is to accustom the body to doing without the drug. This can be accomplished by very gradually reducing the dose—a weekly reduction of 5 mg may be sufficient. Some people can withdraw from the drug quickly, but others may need to proceed more cautiously, especially when the dose approaches zero. During this time there may be shakiness, jitteriness, sleeping difficulties, and increased levels of anxiety, but these symptoms can be minimized by maintaining a very slow pace of drug reduction. Some of the anxiety and sleeping problems may indicate a return of the symptoms that first led to the prescription of the drug rather than the development of withdrawal signs. While the withdrawal signs should disappear one or two months after the last Valium pill is taken, the original anxiety or other problems may persist. The patient and the physician must then decide how best to treat these problems. The alternatives include a resumption of the medication, with the likelihood that dependence will return; use of the medication

A return of the anxiety that led to the use of Valium in the first place may accompany withdrawal from the drug. This may prompt a person to seek drug-free alternatives as a means of relaxing. One option is yoga, a system of exercises derived from Hindu philosophy for attaining physical and mental well-being.

on an occasional basis; or a switch to nondrug therapy.

In most cases patients withdrawing from Valium do not feel a strong desire to resume use of the drug. Although the symptoms that originally led to taking the drug may return, patients may prefer to try other forms of treatment because of their concern about dependence.

Besides being relatively easy to treat, Valium dependence can be avoided fairly easily. The physician should be certain that each patient is taking the smallest dose necessary to alleviate the symptom, such as anxiety. If the anxiety is due to a temporary situation, the drug therapy should stop as soon as the situation has been resolved. If the anxiety is of a more long-lasting nature, the physician should require frequent two- or three-day "drug holidays." During these periods no drug should be taken, and nondrug treatment used if necessary. In addition to helping prevent dependence on the tranquilizer, these holidays help give patients a feeling of being able to control their emotions without the aid of a drug. By inserting drug holidays into the treatment program, by keeping the doses of Valium to a minimum, and by keeping the treatment time as short as possible, the physician decreases the chances that patients will develop a dependence on the drug.

Tranquilizer Abuse

If dependence is considered to be a physiological change resulting from long-term drug intake, abuse can be defined as behavioral changes resulting from drug use. These changes are not the direct result of a drug's actions on behavior, such as ataxia (staggering) or sleepiness, but are only indirectly caused by use of the drug. The abuse of a drug produces drug-seeking behavior. If the drug is illegal or available only by prescription, the behavior might include buying from illicit drug dealers, getting prescriptions for the same drug from several physicians, or altering a prescription so that larger amounts of the drug can be obtained.

Obviously, not everyone who uses drugs of abuse is a drug abuser. Alcohol is clearly a drug of abuse, but the person who drinks primarily on social occasions or who has a beer after mowing the lawn on a hot day is not a drug abuser. If alcohol were no longer available, that person could do without it with little difficulty. People who drink substantial amounts of alcohol daily and who would be greatly distressed if alcohol were not legally available might resort to illegal means to obtain their supply. Such individuals are considered drug abusers. Heavy smokers who are very uncomfortable when they cannot have a cigarette and who would, if necessary, go to a great deal of effort to obtain cigarettes, can also be called drug abusers.

A critical component of drug abuse is the tremendous amount of control that the drug exerts on behavior. Of course, human behavior can be controlled by substances other than drugs. For example, if water were difficult to obtain, a great deal of an individual's behavior would be involved in procuring it. The difference between water and drugs is that the former is a true necessity of life, while the latter is (in many cases) an artificial, or "created," necessity. In addition, unlike water, drugs can have detrimental effects on the individual and on society. Drugs may produce such harmful effects as liver or lung disease, aggressive behavior, poor work habits, and dangerous driving. Drug abuse, then, involves a drug's frequent administration, its potential for controlling behavior, and the potential harm it can cause to the individual and society.

If drug addiction is defined as a compulsive urge to continue using a drug, then smokers who become uncomfortable when deprived of cigarettes and who would go to great lengths to get them can logically be considered drug addicts.

A word that frequently comes up in discussions of Valium is *addiction*. This term has not been used in this discussion because it has never been given an adequate or unambiguous definition. Many people equate addiction with dependence. Others, who focus on drug-seeking and drug-craving behavior, consider addiction to be more closely related to abuse. Because both dependence and abuse are much more clearly defined than addiction, these two terms are used when discussing the potential problems associated with the use of benzodiazepines.

Is Valium a frequently abused drug? Because Valium is so easy to obtain, it is difficult to determine how much effort its users expend on obtaining it or how much effort they would expend if it were more difficult to obtain. It is necessary to examine the overall patterns of Valium use in order to see whether the behavior of Valium users resembles what is recognized as abuse.

Most patients who have received new prescriptions for Valium tend to take less than the amount prescribed by their doctors. Most stop taking the drug on their own after a few weeks, although some may take it again for short periods at a later time. A small percentage of these patients continue to

In 1979 Senator Ted Kennedy, as chairman of the Senate Health subcommittee, presided over a hearing on Valium, then the top-selling prescription drug in the country. The hearing was the government's response to public alarm generated by media reports on an increasing number of cases of Valium dependence and withdrawal.

take the drug on a long-term basis, but very few increase the dose beyond what has been prescribed by their doctors. Even those who do exceed the recommended dose do not appear to use the drug to get high. They are just more likely to feel that they need more Valium to relieve their anxiety than other people do.

Physical dependence on Valium only occurs among people who have taken the drug daily or almost daily for at least two weeks. These people are not necessarily abusing the drug, however. They do not often show drug-seeking behavior but are frequently disturbed by the fact that they become jittery and anxious when their use of Valium is discontinued. Typically, these people want to be free of their need for the drug, and once they are successfully treated for their dependence, they are unlikely to start using it again. Thus, the pattern of use shown by most people who receive a doctor's prescription for Valium is not one that indicates abuse.

Some groups of people, however, do abuse tranquilizers (see Chapter 4). These abusers are usually not people who have sought doctors' prescriptions for Valium to relieve legitimate medical problems. They tend to be people who have already abused other drugs, such as alcohol or barbiturates. The possibility of abusing Valium should be of concern to everyone, but chiefly to those who have exhibited problems with controlling their use of other drugs. There is no evidence indicating that people who take Valium for anxiety will find the drug's effects so pleasurable that they will want to keep taking it just to get high. Therefore, those who use the drug infrequently (or even frequently) because it helps relieve the anxiety or insomnia that disrupts their lives are at little risk of becoming Valium abusers.

The Effects of Valium on Performance

It is difficult for traffic police and emergency-room physicians to determine whether or not Valium is impairing driving ability. Though law-enforcement officials can administer a breathalizer test to determine if a motorist has consumed too much alcohol to drive safely, there is no such test available for Valium. Emergency-room doctors can administer tests to determine levels of tranquilizers in the blood of people involved in traffic accidents, but this procedure is rarely used. The most useful information available on the effects of Valium on driving ability has been obtained by studying how the drug affects those behaviors necessary for safe driving.

More is known about alcohol and driving than is known about most other drugs and driving. A brief outline of the effects of alcohol on driving-related performance will provide perspective for a discussion of Valium's effect on driving. Alcohol, in doses that cause marked impairment in driving ability, does not affect the ability of a person to see or hear. Neither do such doses of alcohol greatly affect the speed or accuracy of a simple response to a visual or an auditory stimulus. Thus, if a person is asked to press a button whenever a light flashes, that person can do it nearly as quickly and accurately when moderately intoxicated as he or she can when sober. However, when the task is more complicated, alcohol's effects become readily apparent. If a mildly drunk person is asked to do two things simultaneously—for example, press a button when a light flashes and step on a pedal when a second light comes on—the individual will perform much more poorly than when he or she is sober. This type of test, called a "divided-attention test," measures an individual's ability to respond to some of the complex situations that frequently arise while driving an automobile.

Much like alcohol, Valium can seriously impair driving ability. It often produces drowsiness and slows a person's reaction time. A driver who combines Valium and alcohol is at high risk of having an accident.

The results from divided-attention tests measuring the effects of Valium have shown that this drug affects behavior in a manner very similar to alcohol. A 15 mg dose of Valium given daily for nine days was capable of disrupting performance significantly. Thus, one may conclude that, like alcohol, benzodiazepines can disrupt an individual's ability to drive. As discussed at the end of this chapter, a driver who simultaneously consumes Valium and alcohol jeopardizes his or her own safety as well as the safety of any passengers and of everyone else on the road.

The effects of tranquilizers on non-driving-related tasks have also been studied. In fact, hundreds of different tests of performance have been used to evaluate many of the anti-anxiety drugs, and from these studies some generalizations can be made. One is that the first few times these drugs are ingested, they produce a sedative effect—sleepiness and a general slowing of responses. But as a person continues to take the medication, this sedative effect decreases. This may be because the body grows accustomed to this effect, because the person learns how to adjust to it, or both. However, the body appears to make much less of an adjustment to the drug's ability to reduce anxiety. This means that someone who takes a tranquilizer for this purpose may experience an unacceptable amount of sedation for the first few days. After

Childbirth Education Association table at a Women's Rights Fair in Philadelphia. Although further research into Valium's effects on the fetus is necessary, the available evidence suggests that Valium increases the chances of birth defects, especially if taken during the first three months of pregnancy.

a while, the sedative effect will become less noticeable, but the drug will continue to control the anxiety.

There is evidence that average doses of benzodiazepines impair the memory and that very high doses considerably increase this effect. This accounts for the use of some of these drugs as pre-operative medication—surgeons do not want their patients to remember any pain involved in their operations. Valium and Librium are two examples of benzodiazepines that produce amnesia (loss of memory) about events following their administration.

Minor tranquilizers do not appear to have much effect on such mental functions as the ability to do arithmetic, to speak and write, or to see and hear. There is also no reason to suspect that these drugs have any effects on mental ability beyond the period of their administration.

Valium and Pregnancy

Valium and other minor tranquilizers are taken by a large number of women, many of whom are in their childbearing years. Therefore, Valium's effect on the unborn child is an

At present, no evidence exists that drug dependency occurs in babies of women who have used Valium. However, considering the unborn child's vulnerability to drugs of any sort, it would be wise to refrain from taking drugs like Valium during pregnancy.

important issue. Unfortunately, there have been few good studies of the effects of Valium or the other minor tranquilizers on the fetus. The small amount of available evidence indicates that when taken during pregnancy, these drugs may increase the chances of birth defects, especially if the drug is taken during the first three months of pregnancy.

In addition to being concerned about birth defects, one must consider the possibility that if the mother is using a minor tranquilizer, the baby will be born with a dependence on the drug. Earlier in this chapter, it was noted that dependence on Valium appears to develop in some people taking only low doses. Although it would seem possible that the baby of a woman who had taken Valium during pregnancy might have a dependence on the drug, and might, therefore, develop withdrawal signs after birth, there are no data indicating that this occurs. However, given the fact that women who take Valium may be at risk, as may their children, both the issue of birth defects and of drug dependence in the newborn infant are greatly in need of thorough study.

Although the question of the effects of Valium on the unborn child has not yet been answered, there are some commonsense points that should be considered. One is that an unborn child is particularly vulnerable to virtually all drugs taken by the mother. The fetus grows extremely rapidly, particularly in the first three months after its conception, when its organ systems are forming and developing. Therefore, an expectant mother should avoid all but the most necessary and thoroughly understood drugs. Since in most cases Valium is not an essential drug, it is wise to be on the safe side and not use it. Another point to keep in mind is that the first three months of pregnancy is also the time when the mother is least likely to be certain, or even aware, that she is pregnant. It is therefore important that any woman who even *thinks* she might be pregnant should take particularly good care of her health by eating well and avoiding all unnecessary drugs.

Combining Valium and Alcohol

Many people who take Valium are also using other drugs. Unfortunately, there have been few studies that have focused on the problems that can arise when other prescription medicines are taken with the minor tranquilizers. However, the dangers of taking Valium in combination with another popular drug, alcohol, are quite clear. There are many similarities between the minor tranquilizers and alcohol. They both have similar negative effects on an individual's driving ability and are capable of reducing anxiety. Furthermore, the body reacts to them in similar ways. It is not surprising, then, that combining Valium and alcohol is more dangerous than using either of these drugs alone. People who drink alcohol and drive are at high risk, and the risks for those who take Valium and drive are probably also increased. When these two drugs are taken together, the danger is even greater. Even a small amount of alcohol can produce intoxication in someone who has taken a single Valium pill.

Another danger connected with this combination is that of overdose. Because it is difficult to consume a fatal amount of alcohol without passing out first, few people die from an overdose of alcohol alone. Likewise, it is difficult to take a fatal amount of Valium. But it is not at all difficult to die from a combination of alcohol and Valium. This can happen not only to people trying to commit suicide, but to those who, unaware of the dangers of ingesting these two drugs in combination, take large amounts of both. It is important that physicians and pharmacists warn patients, both verbally and on the label of the Valium prescription bottle, not to mix Valium and alcohol.

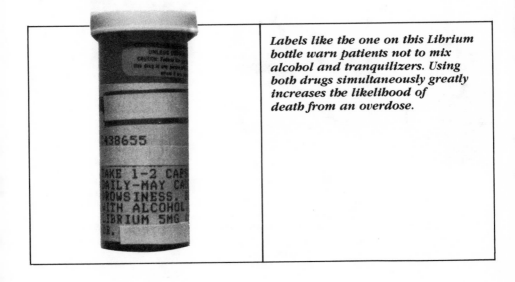

Labels like the one on this Librium bottle warn patients not to mix alcohol and tranquilizers. Using both drugs simultaneously greatly increases the likelihood of death from an overdose.

Tranquilizer use is highest among the elderly, who are also most likely to take the drug for an extended period of time. In every age group, twice as many women as men use tranquilizers.

CHAPTER 4

PATTERNS OF TRANQUILIZER USE

*I*n determining who uses minor tranquilizers and how they use them, a branch of scientific study called epidemiology is utilized. Epidemiology is a science that deals with the incidence, distribution, and control of disease in a population. Epidemiologists conduct surveys of large population groups, asking representative members about their use of drugs. The people surveyed are selected either at random or because they fall into a special group—for example, a group of people that has received prescriptions for benzodiazepines. Surveys of this type have also been given to physicians to determine their prescribing practices and to pharmacists to determine the number of sales of the particular benzodiazepines they dispense.

In 1976 one of the largest of these surveys questioned people in seven countries about their use of medicines. Researchers went to the homes of selected people and asked if they had used any prescribed medication on that day or the previous day. An average of 1.9% reported that they were currently taking a sedative or a minor tranquilizer (for example, Valium, Librium, Miltown, phenobarbital, or an antihistamine). In the United States the average was 2.2%.

A similar survey conducted in western Europe in 1974 asked about the use of minor tranquilizers or sedatives during the preceding 12 months. Of the people questioned, 14% said that they had used such medication in that period, a figure close to the 12% obtained in the United States in 1970 and 1971. Data obtained in a 1979 survey in the United States showed little change in the use of minor tranquilizers over the intervening eight years. Of the U.S. population, 11% had used a drug to reduce anxiety in the preceding year, and 86% of these medications were benzodiazepines. This means that 9.5% of the adults in the United States, or about 15 million people, had used a tranquilizer at least once in 1978.

What type of person takes this medication? Stated somewhat differently, what type of person goes to a physician with an anxiety or insomnia problem? One of the most striking facts about benzodiazepine users is that women outnumber men by as much as 2 to 1. Another striking fact is that the use of these drugs increases considerably in older people. Both of these facts were true in the United States and in each of the other countries studied. Older people are also more likely to use the benzodiazepines for a longer period of time. (The markedly greater tranquilizer use by older people and by women will be discussed in later sections of this book.)

Given that a person took a minor tranquilizer in 1978, what was his or her probable pattern of use? The data indicate that most people used these drugs only occasionally. Of the users questioned, 45% said they took the drug for only a day or two at a time; 20% indicated daily use for longer than 4

The rise of an alienating, uncertain technological culture is considered by some to be the major cause of the anxiety and drug abuse so prevalent in modern society.

months; and 15% reported regular use during the previous 12 months or longer. Although this raises the possibility of abuse in this tranquilizer-using segment of the population, the survey also showed that these people were using the drugs according to their physicians' instructions. They reported higher levels of anxiety and depression, had suffered more setbacks in life, had more problems with their physical health, and saw physicians and psychiatrists more often than those who used the drugs less often. People who took Valium for two weeks or less during the year tended to dislike the side effects of the drug and had generally negative attitudes toward the use of tranquilizers. Thus, it is not likely that these people would abuse Valium.

Do Young People Abuse Tranquilizers?

High school students and even junior high school students appear to be at special risk of taking drugs for nonmedical reasons. In fact, adults who use drugs, including cigarettes and alcohol, usually started using them when they were students. The use of drugs by students is increasing at a rapid rate, and with this expanding use there is growing concern on the part of parents and teachers. Drugs are easily obtained in many schools, and peer pressure often forces a student to try almost any available substance. In an effort to better understand this situation, several studies of drug-taking practices in the student population have been conducted.

In this type of study, researchers often ask a sample of high school students, or an entire class in a particular school, which drugs they have tried and how recently they have used them. Frequently, other questions are also asked in an attempt to determine why young people are taking drugs and what their attitudes are about drugs and drug use. Of course, these questions are not asked publicly. Students are given questionnaires that they can answer anonymously. They are assured that no one wants—or will even be able—to trace a questionnaire to a particular student. There is always a chance that a student will exaggerate or underestimate the extent of his or her drug use. There is also the chance that a student will not know what drugs he or she has taken and will thus not be able to answer the question with any certainty. Absolute accuracy, therefore, is impossible.

The results of one major survey showed that high school seniors do take Miltown, Valium, and Librium recreationally. Approximately 15% of the students surveyed had tried minor tranquilizers at some time during their lives; about the same number said they had tried sedative or hallucinogenic drugs. Approximately half of these users had tried tranquilizers on only one or two occasions. A little over 5% of the students had used tranquilizers during the previous year, and 2.5% had used them within the last month. Although virtually none of the students had used minor tranquilizers on a daily or near-daily basis, 1.7%, or approximately 20 million high school seniors, appeared to have used them on at least 20 occasions in their lifetime. Since drug-use studies in this group began, there has been a gradual decline in the use of tranquilizers by high school seniors. In 1977, 11% indicated that they had taken tranquilizers, but by 1981 this figure dropped to 8%.

This pattern of tranquilizer use is very similar to the reported use of such hallucinogens as LSD and mescaline. The use of these drugs is considerably less than the use of

A young woman smoking a marijuana cigarette. According to studies, fewer high school students have tried tranquilizers (15%) than smoked marijuana (60%), one of the indicators that the abuse of tranquilizers by young people is not particularly common.

alcohol (92.6% of the high school seniors had tried alcohol at least once), cigarettes (71%), or marijuana (59.8%). Careful questioning also revealed that tranquilizers, along with cigarettes, were the only substances of abuse that were not taken by students to produce a high. Because the survey did not attempt to find out what prompted students to take tranquilizers, why this group uses them remains unclear.

Drug-use surveys indicate that boys generally use more drugs than girls do. (Over time, this difference has somewhat decreased.) However, most surveys indicate that girls are more likely than boys to take tranquilizers. This trend is the same among adults, even though adults acquire these drugs by prescription and students generally get them without a prescription.

Questionnaires on student drug use indicate that abuse of tranquilizers is not particularly prevalent among young people. Considering the ease with which these drugs can be obtained, this suggests that the danger of tranquilizer abuse among young people is no greater than the danger of such abuse among adults. Abuse does occur, but it is apparently uncommon and does not seem to be increasing.

Some surveys of students have attempted to find out what factors lead to drug use among young people. One theory is that drug use by children is directly related to drug use by their parents. Fathers of young drug users are likely to drink alcohol, although they are not necessarily alcoholics or even heavy drinkers. Mothers are likely to be frequent users of prescription drugs, including tranquilizers and diet pills. This suggests that illegal drug use by young people may be related to their growing up in an environment in which the taking of legal drugs is common and accepted.

Tranquilizers and the Elderly

Virtually all surveys of benzodiazepine users indicate that the rate of use increases as age increases. There is also evidence that the drug's effects last longer in the elderly and that older people take these drugs for longer periods of time than younger people do. The elderly are faced with many problems that may produce anxiety, and the benzodiazepines can help overcome them. Some of these problems are loss of loved ones; fear of dying; change in financial status; illness with its accompanying pain and anxiety; a feeling of inadequacy now that they are no longer considered to be contributing members of society; more leisure time for which they may not be prepared; and the decreased need for sleep that comes naturally with age.

The dilemma is that many of these problems are inherent to growing old or are built into the social system, so they do not just go away. Is it appropriate for a physician to give a tranquilizer to an 80-year-old man who complains that he cannot sleep eight hours each night when the doctor knows that 80-year-old men normally sleep only six hours each night? The doctor can explain that the decreased need for sleep is normal and counsel the patient to get regular exercise, avoid daytime naps, keep to a daily schedule, and find a hobby to keep himself busy. But these measures may not succeed in helping the patient to adjust to his altered need for sleep. Is it ethical, then, to prescribe a sleeping pill?

There is fairly general agreement that it is entirely ethical to give a pain-ridden terminal-cancer patient all the narcotics he or she needs. The object is to keep the patient as comfortable as possible. The difference between the cancer pa-

Illness, the fear of death, losing friends and family, financial worries, and the threat of being institutionalized can all cause anxiety in senior citizens. Physicians must decide whether tranquilizers will help or hinder the older person's ability to cope with these problems.

tient and the old man is that the cancer patient is suffering from a physical disease and the old man is experiencing an inability to adjust psychologically to a change in life. Some would say that because this latter condition is considered "normal," it is inappropriate to prescribe drugs for the old man. Others would recommend that he be given enough sleeping pills to make his life comfortable. This is a very difficult problem, and the physician may need to do some soul-searching before deciding on the appropriate path to follow.

The problem is even more difficult in traditional nursing homes, where the opportunities for engaging in hobbies or socially useful tasks may be even further reduced and the health of the institutionalized individual is poorer than that of older people who live at home. Should the elderly in nursing homes be given benzodiazepines to help them deal with the fear of dying and to reduce the pain produced by the loss of things that were important to them? Ultimately, younger members of society must be more concerned about the elderly and produce a set of alternatives more satisfactory than mental pain or drug-induced oblivion.

The effect of tranquilizers on the anxieties of the elderly is not as potent as is social interaction, such as time spent with young people.

Drug Abuse

People who obtain tranquilizers through legal prescriptions rarely take more than the prescribed amount and infrequently ingest the drugs for the high they produce. Studies have been made comparing these people with individuals who abuse other drugs in order to learn whether abusers of alcohol and other drugs are more likely to misuse benzodiazepines. However, because there are very few such studies, it is difficult to draw conclusions.

One investigator made benzodiazepines available to a large group of alcoholic patients and recorded the number who showed signs of abusing these drugs. Abuse was defined as an increase over time in the number of pills that these patients took. The observation period ranged from four weeks to over one year. Of the 111 patients who had access to Librium, 7 demonstrated a tendency to abuse it. Of 302 patients to whom Valium was made available, 11 increased their intake over time. Of these 11, 7 had prior histories of sedative and/or narcotics abuse in addition to their abuse of alcohol. These data suggest that alcoholics are not likely to abuse benzodiazepines.

What about people who abuse barbiturates? There have been a number of very careful laboratory studies to determine which of several drugs sedative abusers prefer. The results indicate that sedative abusers show a marked preference for barbiturates over any dosage of minor tranquilizers. However, these people may choose to take benzodiazepines if the other alternative is a placebo. When they do select a benzodiazepine, they pick one that takes effect quickly, such as Valium, in preference to one that works more slowly, such as oxazepam (trademarked Serax). Although it would be useful to know how often sedative abusers take benzodiazepines outside the laboratory, this research has not yet been done. Because barbiturates are not difficult to obtain, it seems unlikely that users of these drugs would choose to use or abuse the benzodiazepines.

One group of drug abusers who have been found to use Valium as a preferred drug are narcotics addicts who are being treated with methadone. Methadone is a narcotic that reduces the addict's need for other narcotics such as heroin. With this need reduced, patients have less motivation to steal in order to support their drug habit, and they can hold a regular job and be an asset to society rather than a drain on its resources.

Clients of legal methadone clinics are required to submit urine samples on a regular basis to prove that they are not also taking street drugs. In 1981, two methadone clinics independently noted that the urine of several of their clients contained benzodiazepine. When questioned, the clients reported that ingesting Valium after a dose of methadone boosted methadone's effects. Interestingly, barbiturates did not seem to have this effect. Neither is there any report of Valium boosting the effects of heroin. The methadone clients reported taking very high doses of Valium (as much as 100 mg per day, as compared to the therapeutic dose of 2 mg to 10 mg per day). It is not yet known whether Valium actually increases methadone's effects or whether combining the two drugs is just a passing fad. Clearly, research using both humans and animals is needed to help explain the popularity of this drug combination.

Clients of methadone clinics (methadone is a narcotic used in heroin withdrawal) must submit urine samples regularly to prove they are not taking other drugs. In 1981, two clinics found urine containing traces of benzodiazepine in several clients who said Valium increased methadone's effects. There is no evidence to support this claim.

Joggers stretching their leg muscles before a run. Daily exercise such as running is an excellent temporary release for excess energy generated by the body's reaction to anxiety.

CHAPTER 5

COPING WITH ANXIETY: TRANQUILIZERS AND THEIR ALTERNATIVES

Different people get anxious for different reasons, and therefore it is difficult to prescribe a general therapy for reducing all anxiety. However, in cases where the anxiety is being caused by an identifiable problem, the most obvious approach is to get rid of that problem. While this is not always easy or even possible, it should always be the first solution considered.

Parents who are anxious, irritable, and frequently upset with their children may be wiser to take a break than to take a Valium. A friend or baby-sitter, by giving the tense parent some time to him- or herself, can sometimes relieve a surprising amount of pressure. People suffering from anxiety because of their work or coworkers should seriously consider looking for another job. Even if getting a new position means going to night school or earning somewhat less money, in most cases it would be better than using drugs to cope with the difficulties. This is not because drugs always pose health risks, but because they do not solve the real problem.

Talking to a Friend

In many cases of anxiety, a person may be so overwhelmed with a problem that he or she cannot see a way out or even be sure there is a way out. One of the best ways to deal with anxiety is to talk to someone. A professional counselor can be quite helpful if friends and family are not available or interested. If the problems are severe, a counselor may even be a necessity. But frequently a sympathetic friend can be as beneficial as a professional. The simple process of talking can be extremely helpful. Trying to explain your difficulty to someone else can help make sense of it and/or put it into perspective. By attempting to make yourself clear, you distance yourself from your emotions and thus are better able to define the contributing causes of the problems, and talk about why you are so disturbed by the situation. This seemingly simple approach may lead to your discovering a solution to the problem, something that no drug can do by itself.

Physical Therapies

If the problem occurs repeatedly and is not relieved by counseling and advice, it may be helpful to find a temporary solution that will provide some anxiety-free periods each day. One excellent short-term solution is to develop a daily exercise program that demands enough energy and attention to provide a break from whatever it is that is producing the anxiety. Anxiety can trigger a release of the hormones that increase heart rate and blood pressure, which, in turn, can help a person escape from danger. This is important if the

Another method of alleviating the physical tension caused by anxiety is swimming, which relaxes, invigorates, and loosens tight muscles.

individual must run away from something, such as an animal or an assailant, but it is not very useful if the person leads a sedentary existence in an office or in the house. Exercise helps to use up the extra energy produced by the release of these hormones. In addition, by loosening tense muscles, exercise promotes relaxation.

Anxiety frequently finds its way into one's jaw, neck, shoulders, and back, where it can squeeze the muscles into tight bunches. Relaxing these muscle contractions can often relieve anxiety. It is not a coincidence that the benzodiazepines, which are very good at reducing anxiety, are also very good at relaxing muscles. However, if relaxation can be produced by nondrug means, then the sedation that often accompanies drug use can be avoided, and a feeling of being able to control one's own muscles—and one's anxiety—may be gained.

Massage is an effective and pleasant way to reduce muscle tension, but unfortunately it is not always available. Neck exercises, which can be done without the assistance of another person, can often help. Another technique is also frequently useful. If you are feeling particularly tense or anxious, take a few minutes to concentrate on those muscles that feel tight. Put everything out of your mind except those muscles. This may be the first time you realize how tight they actually

Often the best way to deal with anxiety is to discuss it with a friend. Talking about a problem can define its cause and put it in perspective.

are. Think about the tense spots and concentrate on trying to relax them. Try tightening them even more and then relaxing them. This will help you to identify your problem areas and will give you more control of the muscles involved.

At first, this technique may not seem to produce any results. But it is probably not a good idea to work too hard at it all at once or at any one time. Ultimately you will develop a quick, effective way to calm anxiety that can be used virtually anywhere, anytime. By working on the worst muscles for brief periods on a daily basis, it should become possible to isolate and reduce the tension before it reaches uncomfortable levels.

Dealing with Insomnia

Difficulty in falling or staying asleep, whether it is occasional or persistent, is extremely distressing to many people. Like anxiety, insomnia tends to feed on itself—the more difficult it is to fall asleep, the more concerned a person gets, and the more concerned a person gets, the harder it is to fall asleep. There are several techniques that can reduce insomnia. One is not to worry about it. It is very useful to keep in mind that one can survive for short periods with insufficient sleep. An individual may not feel particularly refreshed and alert on a day following a sleepless night, but neither performance nor appearance is likely to be dramatically changed. It is not a good idea to start driving on a long trip without plenty of sleep, but with regard to most daily tasks, such as those necessary for schoolwork, housework, and business, with a little effort it is possible to overcome any minor ill effects produced by lack of sleep. With this in mind, a person will probably worry less when sleep problems arise, and this in itself may make sleep possible.

Sleep comes most easily when a person is thinking about pleasant, relaxing things. When bedtime thoughts turn to daily problems and troubles, these must be replaced with thoughts that do not provoke anxiety. Thus, "counting sheep" is the most well-known diversion for those who are trying to go to sleep. Though sheep counting in particular does not work for many people, the general idea is a good one. Thinking about pleasant subjects works fairly well for most people. Bedtime is the time of day for daydreaming. Envision in detail making the game-winning home run in a neighborhood soft-ball game; contemplate the pleasure of catching the attention of an attractive man or woman. Sexual fantasies, if they are relaxing, are appropriate and helpful at this time. If pleasant thoughts are hard to hold onto because of overriding anxiety, look for a more rigorously defined task to think about. Try naming all 50 states in the United States in alphabetical order; when this is mastered, try putting the capital city with each state. If one's thoughts are not sufficiently sleep-inducing, someone else's might be. Watching television or listening to a talk show on the radio are effective sleep inducers for some people. Those who are particularly lucky may have a friend who is willing to read them to sleep.

If you go to bed and are unable to fall asleep, do not stay in bed. Get up, go somewhere else, read a book, watch television, or listen to quiet music. If you stay in bed night after night, frustrated by the fact that you are awake, the bed can become associated with an inability to sleep, which can lead to chronic insomnia. Insomnia caused by this association can often be alleviated by sleeping in a different environment.

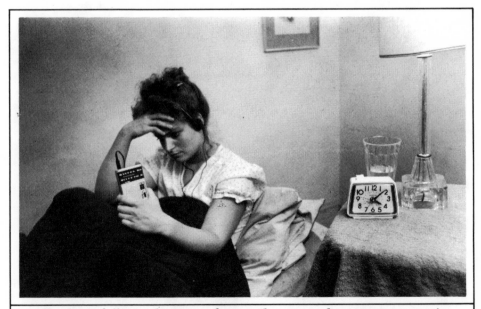

Difficulty in falling asleep most frequently occurs when a person worries about daily concerns once in bed. Drug-free methods to relieve insomnia include reading and listening to quiet music.

The change to a different bed, a different room, or even a sleeping bag on the floor can help sleep come surprisingly quickly and easily.

Psychotherapy

Treatment of anxiety and other psychological disorders is frequently the task of psychiatrists. Thirty years ago, these physicians knew little about the biological factors underlying psychological disorders, and they had access to very few medicines with which to treat them. The most common method of treating psychiatric patients was simply to listen to them. From these listening sessions the psychiatrist would try to determine what problems—conscious or unconscious—were causing the patient's distress and would then try to help the patient recognize and deal with the problems. Once the problems were understood, the patient, it was reasoned, would be able to deal with them in a satisfactory way. Today there is a wide variety of drugs with which many mental diseases can be successfully treated, and the task of listening to and directing emotionally troubled patients has fallen largely to psychotherapists, psychologists, and those psychiatrists who continue to feel that this is the most appropriate treatment.

The supportive environment of therapy groups can often help people deal with their anxieties and cope more effectively with stress.

There has been considerable controversy about the success of psychotherapy. One of the difficulties in measuring its success arises from the fact that most supporters of psychotherapy feel that any interaction between doctor and patient is both private and unique. Therefore, they consider it inappropriate to evaluate the outcome of such an interaction by applying generalized scientific methods. Those who question the use of psychotherapy reply that if the therapist cannot or will not prove that his or her therapy works, no one should be foolish enough to use it. It is unlikely that this issue will be settled in the near future.

Psychotherapy typically requires many months, and sometimes years, of treatment. The high financial cost limits it to patients who can afford it, or who have insurance that covers it. However, psychotherapy can help those anxiety patients who have access to it. It may not be as effective as drug therapy for some types of severe anxiety, but it can be used in conjunction with drug therapy to help patients deal more effectively with their environment.

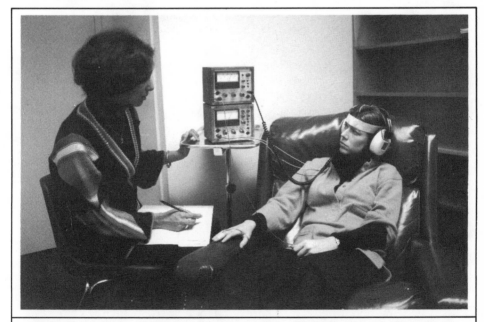

Biofeedback is an attempt to become aware of internal bodily functions usually considered involuntary. Using biofeedback equipment, people can learn to monitor and lower their own blood pressure.

Behavioral Therapy

There are several programs of behavioral treatment for anxiety. Behavioral methods include biofeedback, desensitization, and anxiety management training. These approaches have many similarities. Each attempts to provoke anxiety, make the subject aware of the specific feelings of anxiety in the body, and then teach the subject how to reduce these feelings.

Biofeedback makes use of the increases in blood pressure that are the result of anxiety. Though patients are not usually aware of these increases, scientific equipment can detect the changes and alert the patient by turning on a light. When biofeedback training begins, the patient is asked to lower his or her own blood pressure. Patients are not told how this is done and therefore must find their own way to do it. If they succeed, a light goes on. At first, very small decreases in pressure are rewarded with the light. As the treatment progresses, only significant decreases are rewarded. Over time, patients become very sensitive to changes in their blood pressure and they are able to reduce it with relative ease. When they have reached this level of proficiency, the patients are then capable of using the biofeedback technique to reduce blood pressure and its associated anxiety whenever they occur.

Desensitization, which was described earlier in the treatment of phobias, is used most frequently to treat very specific anxieties. First, the patient learns relaxation procedures and/or methods of gaining a sense of control over any given situation. The patient then concentrates on the object that causes the anxiety and tries to replace the resulting anxious feelings with feelings of relaxation and competency. Once this can be done successfully, the patient proceeds from thinking about the anxiety-provoking object to confronting some mild form of the object itself. A person with fear of flying will first think about flying and then perhaps be shown pictures of an airplane from a passenger's point of view. The patient may then sit in the passenger seat of a grounded airplane and, finally, fly a short distance in the plane. At each of these steps, the patient practices relaxation procedures until he or she is comfortable with and feels in control of the situation.

Anxiety management training (AMT) resembles desensitization, except that it teaches general anxiety reduction rather than specific anxiety reduction. Patients first learn how to identify their anxiety symptoms, such as increased muscle tension, and then learn how to relieve the symptoms. The symptoms of anxiety may be induced by showing horror movies or reading Edgar Allan Poe stories, and relieved by using muscle relaxation techniques.

Behavioral methods are quite effective in treating anxiety such as phobias resulting from specific situations, but they are less helpful in treating generalized anxiety disorders or agoraphobia. Their effectiveness in the treatment of the more normal anxieties from which most of us suffer is not yet certain. The main disadvantages of each of these methods lie in the special training and equipment required to practice them and in the length of time required both to learn the techniques and to apply them. Today, when many people demand quick results with the least amount of effort, these disadvantages may seem insurmountable. But for the individual who is not willing to use or continue drug therapy, the behavioral methods are worth trying.

Desensitization is a treatment for anxieties like aviophobia (fear of flying). The individual confronts the fear step by step, beginning by looking at pictures of planes, and ultimately taking a short flight.

Xanax tablets being manufactured. In 1980, the total wholesale revenue for all minor tranquilizers was $400 million, illustrating that marketing prescription drugs is indeed big business.

CHAPTER 6

ECONOMIC ISSUES AND PRESCRIBING PRACTICES

*T*he exceptional popularity of the minor tranquilizers and controversy surrounding their use have brought much criticism of the companies that reap the profits from the sale of these drugs. Drug companies rarely release information on the specific costs of their research, development, and manufacturing processes, so there are few hard facts available on the cost of producing a drug such as Valium. Because of this, the question of how much profit drug companies actually make on minor tranquilizers is a matter of speculation.

One interesting action occurred in the early 1970s, when Great Britain's House of Commons voted to reduce the price of Librium and Valium on the grounds that the manufacturing company was charging too much for them. The drug company, which almost completely monopolized sales, was charging 40 times the cost of the materials required to make the drugs. The House of Commons went on to recommend that physicians look for other tranquilizers to prescribe for their patients. It even considered forcing the drug company to reimburse patients for their overpayments. The company replied that a very large proportion of its profits went to further research efforts aimed at developing new medications and that only a small proportion went into the pockets of the company's shareholders. Unimpressed with the company's arguments, the government ordered it to reduce the prices of Valium and Librium substantially.

The research and development necessary to develop new drugs is, in fact, very expensive. This expense increases as new legislation requires more and more testing of drugs before they are made available for use by patients. According to current estimates, only 1 of every 10,000 drugs developed by drug companies ever becomes available to the public; it takes 7 to 10 years for a drug to pass all the tests required before it can be put on the market; and the cost of each new drug developed comes to millions of dollars. When Valium and Librium were introduced, the laws were considerably less restrictive than they are now. Therefore, these drugs became available much more quickly and at a lower cost to the manufacturer than if they had been developed today.

Drug companies, like most other businesses in a capitalist system, do everything they can to increase their income, which supports all aspects of the company, including their research efforts, their employers and employees, and, if the company is publicly owned, their stockholders. A widely practiced method of increasing profits is to charge "what the traffic will bear,"—in other words, as much as possible. The ability of a drug company to charge a high price for one of its products is increased when there are no strong competitive drugs on the market. The probability of this being the case is strengthened when the company has patents on its medication and uses every excuse to extend the length of these patents. Ideally, companies would have only the public

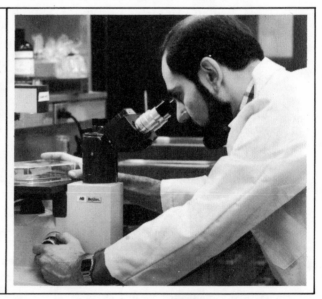

Drug research and development is an expensive and lengthy process. Each new drug costs millions of dollars to develop and requires seven to ten years of testing before it can be approved by the Food and Drug Administration (FDA) and marketed.

good at heart. They would sell their drugs at the lowest possible prices, inform the public of the drugs' potential dangers, and continue to monitor and test their drugs for additional dangerous effects even after the drugs were on the market. Unfortunately, this is not the way the system works.

Companies that produce drugs, like companies that make automobiles, computers, or other products, are interested in investing as little money as possible in their products; selling them for as much as they can; and making as much profit as possible. However, drug companies, like automobile companies, make products that are potentially dangerous. Because in a capitalist economy a company's primary focus is frequently limited to profitability, sometimes at the expense of safety, government agencies and consumer protection organizations must take the responsibility to determine when a product is too dangerous, to publicize their findings, and to lobby among legislators to force the manufacturer to make the product safer. Ultimately, however, consumers who are truly interested in ensuring their health and safety must learn as much as they can about drugs and their manufacturers.

Prescribing Practices

During their first two years in medical school, students receive considerable training in the mechanisms of drug action. They study the reasons for treating specific illnesses with specific drugs and learn about the dangers of the drugs that they may eventually prescribe. When medical students come into contact with patients, they learn the practical aspects of using drugs under the guidance of experienced physicians. However, once they graduate and begin to practice medicine, doctors get their knowledge about new pharmaceuticals largely from the companies that manufacture and sell the drugs.

Drug companies have two methods of telling doctors about their products. One is through advertisements in medical journals and the other is through *detailmen*, or pharmaceutical sales representatives. Medical journal advertising is aimed directly at the physician. It typically provides information about conditions for which the drug can be used, lists any advantages the drug offers over other treatments, describes complications that have followed administration of the drug, and outlines situations in which the drug should not be used or in which it has not been evaluated.

As could be expected from companies in business to make money, the ads are professionally designed by advertising companies. Often in full color, they sometimes fill two or more pages of a medical journal. The drug companies pay the medical journals for the advertising space, which accounts for most of the magazines' income. As a rule, the journals do not evaluate, censor, or endorse the advertisements. However, the U.S. Food and Drug Administration (FDA) has strict rules for drug advertisements. If they are found to be incorrect or misleading, the drug companies are compelled to publish "corrective advertising" in which the errors are pointed out. The companies can also be required to send a letter to every doctor in the country, explaining the mistakes in the advertising. Since such errors can be both expensive and embarrassing, drug companies are very careful about the advertising they publish in medical journals.

Detailmen are hired by pharmaceutical companies to visit physicians. They give the doctors the latest information about the companies' drugs and answer the doctors' questions about the products. Drug companies spend tremendous amounts of money to tell physicians about their products, which is not surprising since the only way that controlled

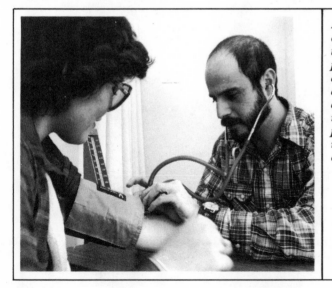

A blood pressure examination. Unlike tranquilizer prescriptions, which, according to statistics, are given to twice as many women as men, blood pressure prescriptions do not reflect a bias toward either sex.

drugs can be legally sold is through doctors' prescriptions. It has been estimated that drug companies spend as much as $7,000 per physician per year in advertising. A large part—perhaps one-third or more—of the average drug company's budget goes toward this advertising.

These large sums of money spent by drug companies to try to influence physicians' prescribing practices are a matter of concern to many people. They are afraid that, in the long run, the profit motive of drug companies may be responsible for inappropriate drug taking. The drugs that cause the most concern are not those that are prescribed to treat readily identifiable symptoms. Antibiotics, analgesics (painkillers), and drugs that reduce high blood pressure, for example, are

At least one-third of the average drug company's budget is spent on advertising their products in medical journals for physicians.

usually prescribed only when a patient's symptoms clearly warrant their administration. Some critics of the drug industry believe that the drug companies' advertising and detailmen are most influential in promoting drugs for conditions whose symptoms are not very clear-cut. These include many of the drugs used for psychological disturbances such as depression and anxiety. Drug companies have been accused of using advertising to "create" illnesses in order to promote their products. Examples of such advertisements are those that appeared in the 1960s and 1970s for Valium. In one ad, the drug was recommended for the high school graduate who is anxious about the dramatic change in life that will accompany going away to college. In another, it was recommended for the young mother who finds her child-care responsibilities burdensome. Medical journals no longer carry such clearly inappropriate advertisements for benzodiazepines. This is due to the FDA's strict rules and to the accumulating evidence that benzodiazepines have potentially dangerous side effects. Advertising that recommends the almost casual prescribing

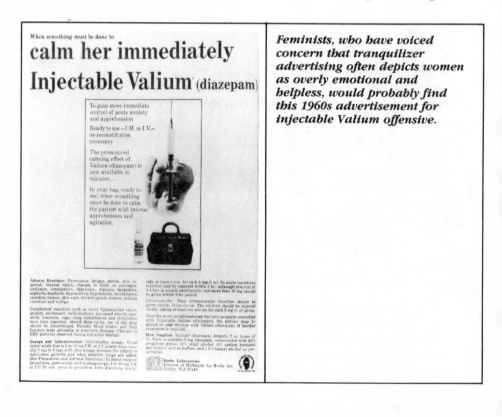

Feminists, who have voiced concern that tranquilizer advertising often depicts women as overly emotional and helpless, would probably find this 1960s advertisement for injectable Valium offensive.

of benzodiazepines would be unacceptable to physicians who are now aware of the hazards posed by these drugs.

How strong an effect advertising has on physicians' prescribing practices is a question that interests the public as well as the advertising and drug companies. Some consumer advocates think it should be illegal for drug companies to advertise their products. They believe that information about new drugs and new uses for old drugs should come from a source that has no connection to the drug companies. Other people argue that most physicians are intelligent people who can make well-informed decisions about drug prescriptions even when the advertising is inappropriate. Since no one knows the effects of advertising on prescribing practices, it is difficult to say which of these positions is more reasonable. In any event, because of legislative and consumer pressure, it appears that some drug companies have changed their advertising approach to reflect current awareness of the dangers of specific drugs.

Studies of physicians' prescribing practices have concentrated on such factors as the physicians' level and recency of education, their general attitudes toward drug therapy, their age and sex, and the age and sex of their patients. The results of such investigations are not surprising. Doctors who have a generally favorable view of the use of drugs for psychological problems are likely to prescribe minor tranquilizers. The research also indicates that there is a large amount of variability in the tendency of physicians to prescribe these drugs. This variability is greater than that found for other types of drugs, even those used to treat emotional and psychological problems. The physician's age and sex, type of practice, and medical experience do not appear to affect his or her prescribing preference. In fact, it is not at all clear what does affect the tendency of doctors to prescribe minor tranquilizers.

Prescribing Tranquilizers: A Feminist Issue?

Benzodiazepines are prescribed twice as often for women as for men. There has been an ongoing discussion about the reasons for this imbalance, and, as a result, several theories have been developed. Statistics show that more women than men visit physicians, and it has been argued that this accounts for the greater prescription of minor tranquilizers for women. There does not appear to be a similar discrepancy between men and women in the prescriptions of antibiotics or medication for high blood pressure, which indicates that factors other than frequency of seeing a doctor may be involved.

Another theory is that men, who are more likely to drink than women (at least partially because it is more acceptable for men to use alcohol), treat their anxiety with alcohol rather than with tranquilizers. It is also possible that in our society women are encouraged more than men to talk about their emotions and to discuss them with their doctors. In other words, women may tell their doctors that they are anxious more often than men do, and are thus more likely to receive treatment for anxiety.

The possibility that most concerns some people is that physicians, being predominantly male, have the biased view that women are more emotionally unstable than men and are therefore more in need of tranquilization. These people argue that male physicians are likely to regard a woman's work as unimportant, which leads these physicians to feel that women will not suffer if their tranquilizer makes them too sedated to go on with their daily tasks. If a male physician sees many female patients who have complaints that have no apparent physical cause and if these women frequently return to his office without appearing to be ill, the doctor may prescribe a tranquilizer just to give them the impression that he is doing something to help them. If, in fact, attitudes like these were to result in the increased frequency of prescriptions of tranquilizers to women, then women would have reason to believe that they were being treated inappropriately.

Though there has been little research on this subject, the data from a few careful studies do not support the theory that physicians are discriminating against women in prescribing tranquilizers. There is also no indication that physicians are more likely to prescribe a tranquilizer for women than for men, given that both present the same complaint. However, more research needs to be done before unchallengeable conclusions can be made.

The possibility that tranquilizer advertising may discriminate against women—by portraying them as emotional, dependent, and helpless, and thus in need of tranquilizers—has been evaluated thoroughly. The results of the studies differ, but the most recent examination of advertisements for tranquilizers indicates that, if anything, men are more frequently portrayed as needing tranquilizers than women.

Finally, it is difficult to state clearly why women take many more tranquilizers than men do and why this discrepancy starts as early as the high school years. Research data do show that tranquilizer use by women is greater among those who work only in the home and among those who are not married. This may reflect a correlation between use of tranquilizers and dissatisfaction with life. It also may mean that finding a job and sources of satisfaction and companionship outside the home increases the quality of a woman's life, and decreases her need for tranquilizers. In addition, it may indicate that to deal with current societal pressure to be married and to work outside the home and to combat their anxiety and feelings of inadequacy, some women resort to using tranquilizers.

There are no conclusive explanations as to why the majority of tranquilizer users are women. Some believe that the current social pressure to have both a career and a family is in part responsible.

Even an average dose of Valium can cause sedation and sleepiness in people unaccustomed to the drug. An overdose, although usually not fatal, is likely to produce long-term sedation and possibly coma.

CHAPTER 7

CONCLUSION

*T*he data that have been gathered in the continuing evaluation of benzodiazepines make it quite clear that these drugs are very effective in the treatment of acute or chronic anxiety, whether it is mild or severe. These drugs are superior to those previously used for anxiety because they are more effective, less likely to be abused, and much less dangerous when an overdose is taken.

The benzodiazepines became extremely popular almost as soon as they became available in the 1960s. Valium was the most frequently prescribed drug in the United States for an entire decade. While the number of prescriptions for Valium and other benzodiazepines has declined since reaching a peak in the 1970s, these drugs are still among the most widely used prescription medicines.

The fact that so many of these drugs are prescribed and ingested has caused considerable concern, both in the medical community and among the people who have received prescriptions for them. While the high rate of use of these drugs could mean that they are an effective treatment for a problem afflicting a large portion of the population, it could also mean that the drugs are being abused, especially if the manufacturers are advertising the use of the drugs for inappropriate reasons or if physicians are prescribing them to patients who do not need them. Studies have been fairly consistent in finding that abuse of these drugs is comparatively rare, however. People who receive prescriptions for benzodiazepines to treat medical problems rarely take more of the medication than their doctors recommend and do not often take it for periods longer than those required to treat their problems. There are certainly cases of benzodiazepine abuse, but considering the number of people who have taken this medication, the number of people who have abused it is quite small.

It is more difficult to determine whether physicians have prescribed the medication inappropriately—for example, to placate patients who make frequent visits with imaginary complaints. This undoubtedly happens to some extent, but it probably accounts for a relatively small proportion of the benzodiazepine prescriptions that are written. It is surely less common now that physicians are aware of some of the dangers of benzodiazepine use.

It is clear that in the past some advertising by drug companies suggested the use of benzodiazepines when the drugs were not warranted. However, due to the criticism brought to bear on the companies, and to the increasing concern about the high levels of benzodiazepine use, in recent years advertising has been more appropriate. It thus appears that benzodiazepines are popular primarily because a large number of people suffer from anxiety and because these drugs are effective in reducing anxiety. The ultimate question,

One type of behavior therapy unites agoraphobiacs into groups who go on shopping trips in an effort to overcome their fear of public places.

which is beyond the scope of this book, is whether this high amount of anxiety is best treated by drugs or by a reorientation of the society that produces the anxiety. The fact that the majority of tranquilizer users are women and senior citizens suggests that these two groups of people may be the objects of social discrimination.

Although abuse of Valium does not appear to be a significant problem, dependence on this drug is a matter of serious concern. Recent findings that therapeutic doses of benzodiazepines, when used over the course of a few weeks, can produce physiological dependence have worried both the public and the medical community. The possibility that these drugs can cause dependence suggests that anyone who has taken them daily for four weeks or more should not stop using them abruptly, but should consult his or her physician for assistance in gradually reducing the dosage.

These drugs are not to be taken lightly. Physicians must carefully monitor their use, and patients must constantly re-evaluate the drugs' benefits and hazards to determine whether drug use should begin or be continued. The benzodiazepines require considerably more respect than they have received in the past.

The fact that women and the elderly comprise the largest percentage of tranquilizer users raises some interesting sociological questions about the nature of anxiety. So far the answers have been highly inconclusive.

APPENDIX 1

HOW TO TELL IF SOMEONE HAS A VALIUM PROBLEM

Most people who take Valium do so to relieve anxiety rather than because it gives them a high. They do not consider themselves drug abusers and so will probably not deny that they are taking the drug. Therefore, the problem is not in discovering whether a person is taking Valium but in deciding whether he or she is having problems related to the use of the drug.

If a parent or a friend seems groggy or sedated, falls asleep at inappropriate times, or has difficulty walking with a steady gait, it could be due to taking too much Valium. Some people who take this drug become aggressive. A sudden personality change that includes an increase in anger or contrariness, or even physical abuse, may indicate that a person cannot handle Valium. This person should be encouraged to have his or her physician prescribe a different type of tranquilizer.

Problems can also result if the person suddenly stops taking Valium. Jitteriness, insomnia, anxiety, tremors, and excessive sweating frequently develop. If this occurs, the best thing to do is to encourage the individual to resume taking Valium and contact his or her doctor so that the Valium withdrawal can be carried out slowly and under medical supervision.

APPENDIX 2

RULES FOR SAFER USE OF VALIUM

1.   Use Valium only for the relief of severe symptoms, not for minor complaints.

2.   Diagnose and treat the underlying disorders before settling for the relief of symptoms.

3.   Remember that drugs are only part of an overall plan of management and treatment.

4.   Avoid taking drugs if you have a history of drug abuse or misuse.

5.   Do not take doses that are so high that your functions are impaired.

6.   Be familiar with the techniques of withdrawal before abuse or misuse occurs.

7.   Be aware of the possibility of dependence whenever you are on long-term treatment.

8.   Learn about the interaction of Valium and alcohol and sedatives.

9.   Do not share Valium with others for whom this drug has not been specifically prescribed.

10.   Keep Valium and all other drugs out of the reach of children.

APPENDIX 3

STATE AGENCIES
FOR THE PREVENTION AND TREATMENT
OF DRUG ABUSE

ALABAMA

Department of Mental Health
Division of Mental Illness and
  Substance Abuse Community
  Programs
200 Interstate Park Drive
P.O. Box 3710
Montgomery, AL 36193
(205) 271-9253

ALASKA

Department of Health and Social
  Services
Office of Alcoholism and Drug
  Abuse
Pouch H-05-F
Juneau, AK 99811
(907) 586-6201

ARIZONA

Department of Health Services
Division of Behavioral Health
  Services
Bureau of Community Services
Alcohol Abuse and Alcoholism
  Section
2500 East Van Buren
Phoenix, AZ 85008
(602) 255-1238

Department of Health Services
Division of Behavioral Health
  Services
Bureau of Community Services
Drug Abuse Section
2500 East Van Buren
Phoenix, AZ 85008
(602) 255-1240

ARKANSAS

Department of Human Services
Office on Alcohol and Drug Abuse
  Prevention
1515 West 7th Avenue
Suite 310
Little Rock, AR 72202
(501) 371-2603

CALIFORNIA

Department of Alcohol and Drug
  Abuse
111 Capitol Mall
Sacramento, CA 95814
(916) 445-1940

COLORADO

Department of Health
Alcohol and Drug Abuse Division
4210 East 11th Avenue
Denver, CO 80220
(303) 320-6137

CONNECTICUT

Alcohol and Drug Abuse
  Commission
999 Asylum Avenue
3rd Floor
Hartford, CT 06105
(203) 566-4145

DELAWARE

Division of Mental Health
Bureau of Alcoholism and Drug
  Abuse
1901 North Dupont Highway
Newcastle, DE 19720
(302) 421-6101

DISTRICT OF COLUMBIA
Department of Human Services
Office of Health Planning and
  Development
601 Indiana Avenue, NW
Suite 500
Washington, D.C. 20004
(202) 724-5641

FLORIDA
Department of Health and
  Rehabilitative Services
Alcoholic Rehabilitation Program
1317 Winewood Boulevard
Room 187A
Tallahassee, FL 32301
(904) 488-0396

Department of Health and
  Rehabilitative Services
Drug Abuse Program
1317 Winewood Boulevard
Building 6, Room 155
Tallahassee, FL 32301
(904) 488-0900

GEORGIA
Department of Human Resources
Division of Mental Health and
  Mental Retardation
Alcohol and Drug Section
618 Ponce De Leon Avenue, NE
Atlanta, GA 30365-2101
(404) 894-4785

HAWAII
Department of Health
Mental Health Division
Alcohol and Drug Abuse Branch
1250 Punch Bowl Street
P.O. Box 3378
Honolulu, HI 96801
(808) 548-4280

IDAHO
Department of Health and Welfare
Bureau of Preventive Medicine
Substance Abuse Section
450 West State
Boise, ID 83720
(208) 334-4368

ILLINOIS
Department of Mental Health and
  Developmental Disabilities
Division of Alcoholism
160 North La Salle Street
Room 1500
Chicago, IL 60601
(312) 793-2907

Illinois Dangerous Drugs
  Commission
300 North State Street
Suite 1500
Chicago, IL 60610
(312) 822-9860

INDIANA
Department of Mental Health
Division of Addiction Services
429 North Pennsylvania Street
Indianapolis, IN 46204
(317) 232-7816

IOWA
Department of Substance Abuse
505 5th Avenue
Insurance Exchange Building
Suite 202
Des Moines, IA 50319
(515) 281-3641

KANSAS
Department of Social Rehabilitation
Alcohol and Drug Abuse Services
2700 West 6th Street
Biddle Building
Topeka, KS 66606
(913) 296-3925

KENTUCKY
Cabinet for Human Resources
Department of Health Services
Substance Abuse Branch
275 East Main Street
Frankfort, KY 40601
(502) 564-2880

LOUISIANA
Department of Health and Human
  Resources
Office of Mental Health and
  Substance Abuse
655 North 5th Street
P.O. Box 4049
Baton Rouge, LA 70821
(504) 342-2565

MAINE
Department of Human Services
Office of Alcoholism and Drug
  Abuse Prevention
Bureau of Rehabilitation
32 Winthrop Street
Augusta, ME 04330
(207) 289-2781

MARYLAND
Alcoholism Control Administration
201 West Preston Street
Fourth Floor
Baltimore, MD 21201
(301) 383-2977

State Health Department
Drug Abuse Administration
201 West Preston Street
Baltimore, MD 21201
(301) 383-3312

MASSACHUSETTS
Department of Public Health
Division of Alcoholism
755 Boylston Street
Sixth Floor
Boston, MA 02116
(617) 727-1960

Department of Public Health
Division of Drug Rehabilitation
600 Washington Street
Boston, MA 02114
(617) 727-8617

MICHIGAN
Department of Public Health
Office of Substance Abuse Services
3500 North Logan Street
P.O. Box 30035
Lansing, MI 48909
(517) 373-8603

MINNESOTA
Department of Public Welfare
Chemical Dependency Program
  Division
Centennial Building
658 Cedar Street
4th Floor
Saint Paul, MN 55155
(612) 296-4614

MISSISSIPPI
Department of Mental Health
Division of Alcohol and Drug Abuse
1102 Robert E. Lee Building
Jackson, MS 39201
(601) 359-1297

MISSOURI
Department of Mental Health
Division of Alcoholism and Drug
  Abuse
2002 Missouri Boulevard
P.O. Box 687
Jefferson City, MO 65102
(314) 751-4942

MONTANA
Department of Institutions
Alcohol and Drug Abuse Division
1539 11th Avenue
Helena, MT 59620
(406) 449-2827

NEBRASKA
Department of Public Institutions
Division of Alcoholism and Drug Abuse
801 West Van Dorn Street
P.O. Box 94728
Lincoln, NB 68509
(402) 471-2851, Ext. 415

NEVADA
Department of Human Resources
Bureau of Alcohol and Drug Abuse
505 East King Street
Carson City, NV 89710
(702) 885-4790

NEW HAMPSHIRE
Department of Health and Welfare
Office of Alcohol and Drug Abuse
   Prevention
Hazen Drive
Health and Welfare Building
Concord, NH 03301
(603) 271-4627

NEW JERSEY
Department of Health
Division of Alcoholism
129 East Hanover Street CN 362
Trenton, NJ 08625
(609) 292-8949

Department of Health
Division of Narcotic and Drug Abuse
   Control
129 East Hanover Street CN 362
Trenton, NJ 08625
(609) 292-8949

NEW MEXICO
Health and Environment Department
Behavioral Services Division
Substance Abuse Bureau   .
725 Saint Michaels Drive
P.O. Box 968
Santa Fe, NM 87503
(505) 984-0020, Ext. 304

NEW YORK
Division of Alcoholism and Alcohol
   Abuse
194 Washington Avenue
Albany, NY 12210
(518) 474-5417

Division of Substance Abuse
   Services
Executive Park South
Box 8200
Albany, NY 12203
(518) 457-7629

NORTH CAROLINA
Department of Human Resources
Division of Mental Health, Mental
   Retardation and Substance Abuse
   Services
Alcohol and Drug Abuse Services
325 North Salisbury Street
Albemarle Building
Raleigh, NC 27611
(919) 733-4670

NORTH DAKOTA
Department of Human Services
Division of Alcoholism and Drug
   Abuse
State Capitol Building
Bismarck, ND 58505
(701) 224-2767

OHIO
Department of Health
Division of Alcoholism
246 North High Street
P.O. Box 118
Columbus, OH 43216
(614) 466-3543

Department of Mental Health
Bureau of Drug Abuse
65 South Front Street
Columbus, OH 43215
(614) 466-9023

OKLAHOMA
Department of Mental Health
Alcohol and Drug Programs
4545 North Lincoln Boulevard
Suite 100 East Terrace
P.O. Box 53277
Oklahoma City, OK 73152
(405) 521-0044

OREGON
Department of Human Resources
Mental Health Division
Office of Programs for Alcohol and
  Drug Problems
2575 Bittern Street, NE
Salem, OR 97310
(503) 378-2163

PENNSYLVANIA
Department of Health
Office of Drug and Alcohol
  Programs
Commonwealth and Forster Avenues
Health and Welfare Building
P.O. Box 90
Harrisburg, PA 17108
(717) 787-9857

RHODE ISLAND
Department of Mental Health,
  Mental Retardation and Hospitals
Division of Substance Abuse
Substance Abuse Administration
  Building
Cranston, RI 02920
(401) 464-2091

SOUTH CAROLINA
Commission on Alcohol and Drug
  Abuse
3700 Forest Drive
Columbia, SC 29204
(803) 758-2521

SOUTH DAKOTA
Department of Health
Division of Alcohol and Drug Abuse
523 East Capitol, Joe Foss Building
Pierre, SD 57501
(605) 773-4806

TENNESSEE
Department of Mental Health and
  Mental Retardation
Alcohol and Drug Abuse Services
505 Deaderick Street
James K. Polk Building, Fourth Floor
Nashville, TN 37219
(615) 741-1921

TEXAS
Commission on Alcoholism
809 Sam Houston State Office Building
Austin, TX 78701
(512) 475-2577

Department of Community Affairs
Drug Abuse Prevention Division
2015 South Interstate Highway 35
P.O. Box 13166
Austin, TX 78711
(512) 443-4100

UTAH
Department of Social Services
Division of Alcoholism and Drugs
150 West North Temple
Suite 350
P.O. Box 2500
Salt Lake City, UT 84110
(801) 533-6532

VERMONT
Agency of Human Services
Department of Social and
  Rehabilitation Services
Alcohol and Drug Abuse Division
103 South Main Street
Waterbury, VT 05676
(802) 241-2170

VIRGINIA
Department of Mental Health and
Mental Retardation
Division of Substance Abuse ˅
109 Governor Street
P.O. Box 1797
Richmond, VA 23214
(804) 786-5313

WASHINGTON
Department of Social and Health
Service
Bureau of Alcohol and Substance
Abuse
Office Building—44 W
Olympia, WA 98504
(206) 753-5866

WEST VIRGINIA
Department of Health
Office of Behavioral Health Services
Division on Alcoholism and Drug
Abuse
1800 Washington Street East
Building 3 Room 451
Charleston, WV 25305
(304) 348-2276

WISCONSIN
Department of Health and Social
Services
Division of Community Services
Bureau of Community Programs
Alcohol and Other Drug Abuse
Program Office
1 West Wilson Street
P.O. Box 7851
Madison, WI 53707
(608) 266-2717

WYOMING
Alcohol and Drug Abuse Programs
Hathaway Building
Cheyenne, WY 82002
(307) 777-7115, Ext. 7118

GUAM
Mental Health & Substance Abuse
Agency
P.O. Box 20999
Guam 96921

PUERTO RICO
Department of Addiction Control
Services
Alcohol Abuse Programs
P.O. Box B-Y Rio Piedras Station
Rio Piedras, PR 00928
(809) 763-5014

Department of Addiction Control
Services
Drug Abuse Programs
P.O. Box B-Y Rio Piedras Station
Rio Piedras, PR 00928
(809) 764-8140

VIRGIN ISLANDS
Division of Mental Health,
Alcoholism & Drug Dependency
Services
P.O. Box 7329
Saint Thomas, Virgin Islands 00801
(809) 774-7265

AMERICAN SAMOA
LBJ Tropical Medical Center
Department of Mental Health Clinic
Pago Pago, American Samoa 96799

TRUST TERRITORIES
Director of Health Services
Office of the High Commissioner
Saipan, Trust Territories 96950

Further Reading

Bargmann, Eve, Wolfe, Sidney M., Levin, Joan, and the Public Citizen Health Research Group. *Stopping Valium and Ativan, Centraz, Dalmane, Librium, Paxipam, Restoril, Serax, Tranxene, Xanax*. New York: Warner, 1983.

Gordon, Barbara. *I'm Dancing as Fast as I Can*. New York: Harper & Row, 1979.

Green, Bernard. *Goodbye, Blues: Breaking the Tranquilizer Habit the Natural Way*. New York: McGraw-Hill, 1982.

Meleville, Joy. *The Tranquilizer Trap and How to Get Out of It*. Glasgow, Scotland: Fontana, 1984.

Glossary

acrophobia an abnormal fear of heights

addiction a condition caused by repeated drug use, characterized by a compulsive urge to continue using the drug, a tendency to increase the dosage, and physiological and/or psychological dependence

agoraphobia previously defined as a fear of open spaces, now used to mean the fear and avoidance of a cluster of situations in which a person feels cut off from his or her point of security, such as home or familiar people

alprazolam a type of benzodiazepine that is known to be effective against depression, marketed under the trade name Xanax

analgesic a drug that produces an insensitivity to pain without loss of consciousness

anesthetic a drug that produces loss of sensation, sometimes with loss of consciousness

anticholinergic drugs drugs that alter the normal communication between neurons by binding to the receptor sites normally used by the neurotransmitter acetylcholine (ACh)

antihistamine a drug that inhibits the action of histamine and thus reduces the allergic response

anxiety an emotional state caused by uncertainty, apprehension, fear, and/or dread that produces such symptoms as sweating, agitation, and increased blood pressure and heart rate

anxiety management training a program of behavioral treatment for anxiety in which patients first learn how to identify their anxiety symptoms, then learn how to relieve them.

axon the part of a neuron along which the nerve impulse travels away from the cell body

barbiturate a drug that causes depression of the central nervous system, generally used to reduce anxiety or to induce euphoria

benzodiazepine a potent reliever of anxiety and insomnia

beta-blocker a drug used to relieve anxiety by blocking some of the effects of norepinephrine, a hormone released by the body during periods of stress

biofeedback a training program designed to develop an individual's ability to control the autonomic, or involuntary, nervous system, and thus allow him or her to relax and even expand consciousness and self-awareness.

bronchodilator a substance that, by expanding the bronchi of the lungs, clears the air passages and aids breathing

buspirone a drug that may be able to relieve anxiety without producing dependence or unpleasant side effects

claustrophobia dread of being in closed or narrow spaces

clorazepate (marketed under the trade name Tranxene) a benzodiazepine that is useful in the treatment of some seizure disorders

dendrite the hairlike structure that protrudes from the neural cell body on which receptor sites are located

desensitization an anxiety-treating method in which the patient concentrates on the source of stress and then tries to replace the resulting anxious feelings with feelings of relaxation and competency

double-blind experiment an experiment to test the effectiveness of a drug in which the individual does not know if what he or she is taking is the drug itself or a placebo

epilepsy a disorder characterized by convulsive seizures and/or disturbances of consciousness that are associated with disturbance of electrical activity in the brain

epinephrine a broncholdilator whose actions relax muscles, stimulate the heart and the central nervous system, and constrict the blood vessels

fear an unpleasant often strong emotion caused by anticipation or awareness of danger

generalized anxiety disorder a type of anxiety that is considered serious because it is not tied to a specific situation and is often long in duration and imaginary in cause.

hallucination a sensory impression that has no basis in external stimulation

hormone a substance, either bodily or synthetic, that circulates in body fluids and produces effects on the activities of specific cells

hypnotic a sleep-inducing agent

Librium trade name for chlordiazepoxide, a benzodiazepine, or minor tranquilizer

LSD lysergic acid diethylamide; a hallucinogenic derived from a fungus that grows on rye or from morning-glory seeds

meprobamate (marketed under the name Miltown) a drug that developed in the 1950s to relieve anxiety, but has since been largely replaced by products with fewer unpleasant side effects

mescaline a hallucinogenic drug found in certain cacti, chemically similar to amphetamine

metabolism the chemical changes in the living cell by which energy is provided for the vital processes and activities and by which new material is assimilated to repair cell structures; or, the process that uses enzymes to convert one substance into compounds that can be easily eliminated from the body

methadone a synthetic opiate producing effects similar to morphine, used to treat pain associated with terminal cancer and in the treatment of heroin addicts

minor tranquilizer a class of anti-anxiety drugs that differ from stronger tranquilizers in that they are taken in smaller doses and do not have as many unpleasant side effects

morphine opium's principal psychoactive ingredient, which produces sleep or a state of stupor; it is used as the standard against which all morphine-like drugs are compared

mysophobia fear of dirt or contamination

narcotic originally, a group of drugs producing effects similar to morphine; often used to refer to any substance that sedates, has a depressive effect, and/or causes dependence

neurotransmitter a chemical that travels from the axon of one neuron, across the synaptic gap, and to the receptor site on the dendrite of an adjacent neuron, thus allowing communication between neural cells

norepinephrine a neurotransmitter in both the central and peripheral nervous system

pathological due to or involving a mental or physical disease

phobia any persistent abnormal fear

physical dependence an adaptation of the body to the presence of a drug, such that its absence produces withdrawal symptoms

physiological related to the processes, activities, and phenomena characteristic of living organisms *placebo*   a substance that is pharmacologically inactive and is used as a control in experiments measuring the effectiveness of another substance, or is administered in order to satisfy the psychological needs of patients

propranolol   beta-blockers marketed under the name Inderal

psychological dependence   a condition in which the drug user craves a drug to maintain a sense of well-being and feels discomfort when deprived of it

receptor   a cell component that combines with a drug to change the function of the cell

sedative   a drug that produces calmness, relaxation, and, at high doses, sleep; includes barbiturates

strychnine   a convulsive drug

synapse   the gap between the axon and dendrite of two adjacent neurons in which neurotransmitters travel

tetanus   an acute disease characterized by muscle spasms and caused by a toxin that is usually introduced through a wound

tolerance   a decrease of susceptibility to the effects of a drug due to its continued administration, resulting in the user's need to increase the drug dosage in order to achieve the effects experienced previously

tranquilizer   a drug that has calming, relaxing effects

Valium   trade name for diazepam, a benzodiazepine or minor tranquilizer

withdrawal   the physiological and psychological effects that occur after the use of a drug is discontinued

Index

abuse *see* drugs, abuse
acrophobia, 21
   see also phobic disorders
addiction, 63
   see also drugs, dependence
advertising *see* drugs, marketing
agoraphobia, 21, 23, 37, 89
   see also phobic disorders
alcohol, 24, 40, 57–58, 75
   abuse, 25–26, 61–62, 64, 78
   driving, effects on, 65–66, 69
   interactions with other drugs, 29, 66,
      68–69
   overdoses, 69
   withdrawal, 26, 44–46, 58–60
alprazolam *see* Xanax
amitriptyline *see* Elavil
amnesia, 67
AMT *see* anxiety management training
anticholinergics, 51
antihistamines, 27, 71
anxiety
   harmful effects, 19–20, 51
   long-term, 22, 33–35
   neurological basis, 41
   pathological forms, 20–23
   physical symptoms, 20–22, 83
   physical therapy, 82–84
   potential benefits, 19
   psychological counseling, 81–82,
      86–87
   short-term, 34
   situational, 22, 34
   treatment
      with drugs, 20, 23–37, 96–99
      without drugs, 23, 35, 37–38,
         81–84, 86–89
   see also benzodiazepines; generalized
      anxiety disorder; phobic
      disorders; Valium
anxiety management training (AMT), 89
   see also behavioral therapy
anxiety state *see* generalized anxiety
      disorder
ataxia, 61
axon, 38
barbiturates, 71
   abuse, 25–27, 44–46, 58, 64, 78–79
   medical uses, 24–25, 43–44

risks, 43–44, 46, 55
   see also benzodiazepines
behavioral therapy, 37–38, 88–89
   see also anxiety, treatment
benzodiazepines, 23, 27
   abuse, 61–64, 73, 78–79, 102–103
   considerations in prescribing, 35–37,
      68, 76–77, 96–99, 103
   deaths, 53
   dependence, 48, 55–61, 68
   discovery, 29
   ease of obtaining, 55, 75
   economics, 91–93
   intellectual ability, effects on, 67
   marketing, 96–99, 103
   mechanism of action, 39–41, 46
   medical uses, 30–31
      as pre-operative sedative, 51, 67
      treatment of anxiety, 30–35,
         96–99, 102–103
      treatment of depression, 31
      treatment of drug withdrawal,
         44–46
      treatment of epilepsy, 50–51
      treatment of insomnia, 31, 43–44
      treatment of muscle spasm, 47–49
   memory, effects on, 67
   patterns of use, 71–73
      by elderly, 72, 75–77, 104
      by students, 74–75
      by women, 72, 97–99, 104
      in United States, 72, 102
   potential risks, 35, 53–69
   pregnancy, effects on, 67–68
   receptors for, 39–40
   regulation, 91, 96
   relative safety, 30, 43, 46, 53–54,
      102
   sedative effects, 66–67
   testing, 32–34
   withdrawal, 58–61
   see also anxiety; Librium; Serax;
      Tranxene; Valium; Xanax
beta-blockers, 28
   see also anxiety, treatment; Inderal
biofeedback, 88
   see also behavioral therapy
buspirone, 29
cerebral palsy, 48–50

see also benzodiazepines, medical
  uses
chlordiazepoxide *see* Librium
cigarettes *see* smoking
claustrophobia, 21
  see also phobic disorders
clorazepate *see* Tranxene
  see also drugs, marketing
delirium tremens (DTs), 44–45, 58
  see also drugs, withdrawal
Demerol (meperidine), 51
  see also narcotics
dendrite, 38–39
dependence *see* drugs, dependence
depression, 31, 37, 58
desensitization, 38, 88–89
  see also behavioral therapy
diazepam *see* Valium
divided-attention test, 65–66
  see also Valium, driving ability
double-blind placebo-controlled
    experiment, 32
  see also benzodiazepines, testing
"drug holidays," 61
  see also benzodiazepines,
          dependence
drugs
  abuse, 26, 29–30, 61–63
  dependence, 25, 27, 29–30, 48,
    56–57
  economics, 91–93
  marketing, 93–97
  withdrawal
    symptoms, 25, 44–45, 57–58
    treatment, 45–46, 60
  see also alcohol; barbiturates;
          benzodiazepines
  see also drugs, dependence
DTs *see* delirium tremens
Elavil (amitriptyline), 37
epidemiology, 71, 73
epilepsy *see* benzodiazepines, medical
    uses
epinephrine, 19
FDA *see* Food and Drug Administration
Food and Drug Administration (FDA), 94,
    96
GABA, 40–41
  see also benzodiazepines, mechanism
    of action

gamma-aminobutyric acid *see* GABA
generalized anxiety disorders, 20–23, 89
  see also anxiety
Gordon, Barbara, 55
heroin, 78
  see also narcotics
Hoffman-LaRoche, 29
House of Commons (Great Britain), 91
I'm Dancing as Fast as I Can (Gordon),
    55–56
Inderal (propranolol), 28
insomnia, 43–44, 64, 84–86
  see also anxiety
Librium (chlordiazepoxide)
  dependence, 53, 58–59
  discovery, 29–30
  economics, 91–92
  medical uses, 23, 45, 51, 67
  patterns of use, 71, 74
  see also benzodiazepines
limbic system, 41
LSD, 74
lysergic acid diethylamide *see* LSD
marijuana, 75
massage, 83–84
  see also anxiety, treatment
meperidine *see* Demerol
meprobamate *see* Miltown
mescaline, 74
methadone, 78–79
  see also narcotics
Miltown (meprobamate), 23, 27, 40, 71,
    74
  see also benzodiazepines
minor tranquilizers *see* barbiturates;
          benzodiazepines
morphine, 51
multiple sclerosis, 48–50
  see also benzodiazepines, medical
    uses
muscle spasm *see* benzodiazepines,
    medical uses
mysophobia, 21
  see also phobic disorders
narcotics, 57–58, 76, 78–79
  see also drugs, abuse
neurotransmitters, 38–39
  see also benzodiazepines, mechanism
    of action
norepinephrine, 19, 28

oxazepam *see* Serax
panic attacks, 21, 23, 37
   see also anxiety
phobias *see* phobic disorders
phobic disorders, 37–38, 89
   simple phobias, 20–21
   see also anxiety
placebo, 32
   see also benzodiazepines, testing
prescribing practices *see* benzodiazepines,
      considerations in prescribing;
      drugs, marketing; Valium,
      considerations in prescribing
propranolol (Inderal), 28
psychotherapy, 86–87
   see also anxiety, treatment
quinazoline N-oxides, 29
receptors, 39
   see also benzodiazepines, mechanism
      of action
schizophrenia, 58
sedatives *see* barbiturates;
      benzodiazepines
Serax (oxazepam), 78
   see also benzodiazepines
simple phobias *see* phobic disorders
smoking, 62, 75
status epilepticus, 50–51
   see also Valium, medical uses
Sternbach, Leo, 29, 40
strychnine, 47
synapse, 38
tetanus, 47–48
   see also Valium, medical uses
tobacco *see* smoking
tolerance, 25, 27

   see also drugs, dependence
tranquilizers *see* benzodiazepines
Tranxene (clorazepate), 31, 51
   see also benzodiazepines
tricyclic antidepressants, 37
Valium (diazepam), 20, 23
   abuse, 63–64, 73, 78–79, 104
   considerations in prescribing, 35–37,
      49, 55, 61, 68
   dependence, 55–61, 68, 104
   dosages used, 54–55, 60
   driving ability, effects on, 64–66, 69
   economics, 91–92
   intellectual performance, effects on,
      67
   interactions with other drugs, 66,
      68–69, 79
   medical uses
     as pre-operative sedative, 51, 67
     treatment of anxiety, 30, 33–35
     treatment of drug withdrawal, 46,
       51
     treatment of muscle spasm, 47–50
     treatment of status epilepticus,
      50–51
   memory, effects on, 67
   overdoses, 53–55, 69
   patterns of use, 71, 73, 75
   popularity, 30, 35, 102
   pregnancy, effects on, 67–68
   short-term effects, 54–55
   withdrawal, 56, 58–61
   see also benzodiazepines
withdrawal *see* drugs, withdrawal
Xanax (alprazolam), 31, 37
   see also benzodiazepines

Gail Winger, Ph.D., is an assistant research scientist in pharmacology at the University of Michigan, where she earned her degrees in psychology and in pharmacology. She was an assistant professor in the department of psychiatry at New York's Downstate Medical Center and The Johns Hopkins Medical School.

Solomon H. Snyder, M.D., is Distinguished Service Professor of Neuroscience, Pharmacology and Psychiatry at The Johns Hopkins University School of Medicine. He has served as president of the Society for Neuroscience and in 1978 received the Albert Lasker Award in Medical Research. He has authored *Uses of Marijuana, Madness and the Brain, The Troubled Mind, Biological Aspects of Mental Disorder,* and edited *Perspective in Neuropharmacology: A Tribute to Julius Axelrod.* Professor Snyder was a research associate with Dr. Axelrod at the National Institutes of Health.

Barry L. Jacobs, Ph.D., is currently a professor in the program of neuroscience at Princeton University. Professor Jacobs is author of *Serotonin Neurotransmission and Behavior* and *Hallucinogens: Neurochemical, Behavioral and Clinical Perspectives.* He has written many journal articles in the field of neuroscience and contributed numerous chapters to books on behavior and brain science. He has been a member of several panels of the National Institute of Mental Health.

Jerome H. Jaffe, M.D., formerly professor of psychiatry at the College of Physicians and Surgeons, Columbia University, has been named recently Director of the Addiction Research Center of the National Institute on Drug Abuse. Dr. Jaffe is also a psychopharmacologist and has conducted research on a wide range of addictive drugs and developed treatment programs for addicts. He has acted as Special Consultant to the President on Narcotics and Dangerous Drugs and was the first director of the White House Special Action Office for Drug Abuse Prevention.